LIFE
OF
FAITH

A Collection of Poems and Outlines

by Ray Zander

ISBN 0-9773498-0-2

Ray Zander
1107 Duncan Circle #104
Palm Beach Gardens, FL 33418
561-626-1475

TABLE OF CONTENTS
Poems

TABLE OF CONTENTS
Outlines & Acrostics

FOREWORD

At the age of eighty Brother Ray Zander wrote his first poem. At eighty-three years young he still gives birth to several poems every week, to the delight of his many friends and church family.

It has been my privilege to call him my friend and mentor. His knowledge of the bible is remarkable, and his zeal to share Christ with lost souls is unabated even after 60 years of active evangelistic ministry.

"Bro. Ray, the bow tie man" as he is affectionately called by the men in the recovery program at Dunklin Camp is Grandpa to a lot of young men that come from broken homes and welcome his visits to the camp where he has a reserved room every weekend.

Bro. Ray is the most giving man I have ever met. He has never taken an offering in any meeting where he has ministered, but he constantly gives to every needy soul and every worthy cause. He is a sanctified (set apart for divine use) channel through which the storehouse of God's provision flows freely. The Lord's Spirit flows through him like an artesian well where thirsty people can find free water.

Ray's poems were first introduced at the Pole Barn churches at *Dunklin* and *Spur On* ministries where they were warmly and sometimes tearfully received because they were so personal and Christ-Centered.

I pray that these poems will bless your hearts as they have ours.

> Mickey Evans
> Dunklin Memorial

INTRODUCTION

Ray McEwen Zander was born to Al and Martha Zander in 1922. Ray had one brother, Doug. Ray graduated from Lower Merion High School (Ardmore, PA) in 1940. Many of Ray's classmates were called to serve in World War II. Shortly after graduating, Ray himself, entered the Navy and served aboard the fleet minesweeper flagship USS Fierce A.M. 97. Ray was wounded twice while in the war. An explosion on the three-inch, fifty caliber, gun caused deafness for three days, burns and internal bleeding. His right hand was injured by a mine. Two navy hospitals ordered amputation, but he had praying parents back home.

Ray was raised in a godly atmosphere, where Bible reading and prayer began each day. The godly life of his parents affected him greatly. His one desire was to know God. Having trusted Christ as personal Savior three days after his twentieth birthday, he immediately sought to win others to Christ.

"The most important event in my life was the night I received the Lord Jesus Christ as my personal Savior. This took place shortly after two High School companions were killed in a car crash near the Villanova Stadium, where we had just won the state championship in Basketball. It rained that night and the temperature dropped below freezing, making the roads like a sheet of glass. The car skidded and struck a tree. Two young people, a brother and sister were killed. This caused me to search the Scriptures where Romans 6:23 revealed to me God's way of salvation."

"The wages of sin is death, but the gift of God is eternal life through Jesus Christ our Lord."

"I received God's gift and He changed my entire life. I now had a relationship with the Lord Jesus Christ."

Ray worked for many years with his father at Zander's Market in Ardmore PA, eventually opening his own food store. His love for the Gospel overshadowed business. One day his father said he was going to retire and leave everything to Ray. Ray replied, "Dad, I found someone who loved me enough to die for me, and I love Him enough to live for Him." His father's reply was, "I pretty much thought that, but I just want you to know that it's all yours if you want it."

Ray began full-time ministry in 1953. He learned to trust fully on the Lord, depending solely upon God's faithfulness. Though he has traveled in thirty-six countries, he has never had a salary or taken one collection in any service. In over fifty years of full-time ministry, Ray has trusted simply in God's faithfulness, which has never failed, even to this day.

Ray preached with J.T. Dickson, Gordon Reager, Paul Plubell, Robert Crawford, George Baldwin, Oswald McLead, Fred Swartz, Ed Richmond, Edwin Meschkat, Bob Beers, Jonathan Brower, Rob Lindsted, and others. He labored in Richmond VA, Dover DE, Las Vegas NV, Key West FL, California, Texas, British Columbia, the Bahamas, and other places.

There were many influential men in Ray's life. Two of whom were Evangelists Sam and Hugh McEwen, his mother's brothers.

Ray learned the value of prayer from his father. As a boy, as far back as he can remember, he saw his father pray for one hour every day.

> During World War II meat was very scarce and many stores failed. When our store sold out of supplies, Dad would go into the back room, get on his knees and pray. Time after time, a truck would drive up and the driver would tell of another store closing. The driver would say, "If you have cash, it's all yours." Dad's answer was, "Bring it in."

> My brother, Doug, sought to be an atheist. One day he came storming in and said, "Somebody's gotta be listening to Pop, this happens all too often." Later in his life, Doug came to know the Lord. I got a letter from him, in which he said,

> *"I'm the happiest man in town today. I have joy within and peace with God, for the first time in thirty-five years. In traveling in various parts of the world, I noticed the figures of the gods always have their hands out to receive, while my God gives life, happiness, forgiveness, joy, healing, love, and meets every need."*

Ray's policy of depending solely upon the Lord's faithfulness in his ministry has brought him into some very interesting situations.

I had my own self-service food store, but business held little interest for me. The Lord was using me in a greater occupation. Wanting to know God better, I soon ventured out on real tests of faith.

Lest men should feel they were contributing toward their salvation, 1 never took one collection in any service. Nor did I tell my parents my need, as I now worked for a living Savior who was able to do exceedingly above all that we ask or think.

Once, I had just finished a two week service on Great Guana Cay, in the Bahamas. I had been in Abaco for months. I had to wash and drip-dry my suits in brackish water, so the threads were starting to come loose. I buried my two suits at Guana, and headed home in a sports coat and slacks. I wasn't aware of how often I wore a coat until a native said, "Man, does you have elbows?" Upon arriving home, I received a phone call from Atlanta, asking if would come and preach the Word there.

Having spent all my money during services in the Bahamas, I finally agreed to go to Atlanta. I knew the mailman would be by at about 10:00 AM, and I'd have a check. It had been several months and I didn't know how much gas was in my car, but I did have $1.03 in my pocket.

At 10:00 AM, I had the car packed, and no mail had arrived. I felt it was essential to keep my commitment, so I said good-bye to mother and dad. They said they had friends in a town I would be passing through. These people had just built a new house with a room for missionaries and preachers. They wanted me to give their friends their love, and spend the night there.

When I arrived at that house, it was locked up tight, so I headed on to Jacksonville, Florida where a cousin lived. She was an x-ray technician at the hospital. After several phone calls, I finally located her. I asked her if I went to the meeting that night, would she go with me. She said she would.

We went to the meeting, where I was asked to speak. After the meeting refreshments were served, and a young man asked me where I was spending the night. His family had just bought a house and he invited me to be their guest, so I returned my cousin to the hospital and accepted the invitation.

The following morning I drove on up I-75. I looked at the gas gage and it was empty. I saw a huge sign, "Stuckey's, four miles," with a big arrow pointing to the right. When I pulled into the gas station, a young boy greeted me. I immediately told him of my turning to Christ. In doing so, I mentioned that I had joined the Merchant Marines to get away from home and preaching.

The boy asked me if I was a minister. Then the boy disappeared and soon a man appeared in the doorway of the Stuckey's. He pointed to a tract rack on the front of his store. I saw a tract titled, *Salvation Through The Precious Blood.*

I was invited in for a big glass of orange juice, and the man said to me, "Do you see the young man to whom you just witnessed? That is our adopted son. He is just out of the penitentiary, and he likes you. Would you come in, have lunch with us, and witness to him?"

I was treated to a full-course meal and shared God's way of salvation. I started to leave, but the man wanted to give me a gift. I was reluctant to take a gift, but I thanked him kindly and told him what a blessing he had been. He then said, "Just a minute mister-please take this check. Early this morning my wife and I got on our knees and asked God to send a born-again Christian to witness to our son. We promised God to give it to whomever He sent. Please take it!"

The $20.00 check filled my tank with gas, and soon I was on my way to Atlanta, praising God for His faithfulness. Upon arrival in Atlanta, I was greeted by Cleave and Betty and shown my room. Betty showed me a coat in the closet and asked me to try it on. Cleave pointed to the trousers and asked if I'd see if they fit. They both fit perfectly.

(I had buried my only two suits on Guana Cay.) No one knew I needed a new suit but God. Cleave and Betty then told me, "As soon as we heard you were coming we went and bought you this new suit."

Events such as this are so common as I learn to trust Him more each day.

Anyone who knows Ray, knows that he always wears a bow tie. Alfred Adams tells of once when Ray was to preach at a meeting. Unknown to Ray, they passed out bow ties to the entire congregation, and asked them to put them on without letting Ray know. When Ray got up to preach and faced the congregation, he was confronted by a whole congregation wearing bow ties. Ray says he just kept preaching without missing a beat. He says:

> **"I just appreciated the appearance of the well dressed men in the congregation."**

Ever since coming to Christ, Ray has had a desire to bring others to know the Savior. When this happens it brings him great joy.

A radio announcer came to know the Lord in Key West and used his position to win others to the Lord.

For three years the Lord gave me the greatest birthday gift anyone could ever ask for. Each March 8th, a person professed faith in Christ.

I was with a man who was dying of cancer. I was there daily for three months and he trusted the Savior, and passed from death unto life.

A woman asked for help several times but never professed. One day she said, "I don't believe I'll ever be saved." I replied, "Neither do I," and headed for my car. She called for help, and found it in the Lord and His redemptive work at Calvary.

A man attended meetings held by Gordon Reager and Paul Plubell. I had been in the area for several months visiting ten homes a day, reading and praying. A man named Bob, attended meetings on the Second Coming of Christ. Having heard of the soon coming Savior, he was awakened to his need for the Savior.

That night it snowed. When he awoke the next morning, he pondered the fact that the snow had come silently while he slept. He realized the Lord could have come just as silently, and he would have been left with no hope. This led to Bob's salvation.

Once Ray was on Harbor Island, in the Bahamas, for Gospel services. It was his first visit there and he was unknown to the people. After doing visitation and Bible study it came time for him to eat. Having no supplies, and being unfamiliar with the island, Ray knew it was time to pray.

Looking down the lane, I saw a young girl coming toward me with something in her hands. Her first words were, "Mommy sent this to you." I pulled back the white napkin and saw a full-course meal. This proved again God's faithfulness in answering prayer. I walked upstairs with the meal, opened the door, got on my knees and thanked God for meeting my need. Now my faith was stronger still. Being one who loved desserts, I asked God if He would provide this also.

I was walking down the road when a man who was bent over walked up to me and thanked me for spending time on the island. He asked if I would accept a gift, and handed me a little brown paper bag closed tightly at the top. Opening it, I found a piece of homemade cake. My heart went out in praise to God once again.

Ray with his parents
Al and Martha Zander

Two Future Poets
Raymond McEwen Zander (left),
William Douglas Zander (right)

Dear Loved One,

With Jesus' help you cannot fail,
Though Satan's armies tempt, assail.
We have a God who's just and strong,
We now to Him by grace belong.

He bought you at the highest cost,
Reached out to you when you were lost.
He's all the Friend you'll ever need.
Trust and obey, you will succeed.

I'm glad to see you serve the Lord,
Learn well to use His mighty Sword.
Have served the Lord since '53,
Never once has God failed me.

I love you much, for you I'll pray,
That close to Him you'll ever stay.
There is no substitute for prayer,
Call day or night, He's always there.

If you look around or perhaps within,
You may be tempted then to sin.
So read your Bible each new day,
It'll change your life and all you say.

Much love because of Calvary,
Ray Zander

Part 1
POEMS

I FOUND FORGIVENESS

Tho scarred with sin and red with shame
My Lord in love and pity came
To free my soul from certain doom
All by the cross and empty tomb

The Word was clear, blood must be shed
So on to Calv'ry He was led
They pierced His hands and feet and side
He won my heart for me He died

The thorny crown, the nails, the spear
The scourge, the spit, the pulled out beard
The mockings, tauntings, smitings too
Brought forth His blood in full plain view

Without that shedding, forgiveness none
Who could endure but God's own son?
He's looking for some servants true
His eye is gazing straight at you.❧

September 2003
(Ray's first poem)

Winner of the *Editor's Choice Award*
For Outstanding Achievement in Poetry
Presented by The International Library of Poetry
May 2004

ADULLAM
David's Hiding Place

When a hiding place was needed God gave Adullam's cave.
What made the place so special was the leader that He gave.
This Man was now rejected but soon would reign as king.
I'll take my place with Him today and all my praises bring.

When we seek a place to gather do we look for a big crowd?
Or can it be our liking is someplace we could feel proud.
David had a gathering of a most unlikely crew.
It was their love for David made them follow and be true.

There were debtors, discontent ones and men in deep distress.
He was God's appointed leader and they did true love possess.
A dark, damp cave seemed not to matter for it was David-
drew them in.
God gave them all protection they were certain they would win.

Would you be willing to give up your rest.
For the One who's always faithful and gives only what is best?
He's rejected right at present His followers may be few.
Reproach and scoffing wait you if you choose to say, "I do."

If God leads you to a pole barn or dark and dismal cave.
Forget the stained glass windows or the preacher's friendly wave.
If Christ is not the center you can't be satisfied.
Turn your eyes right now to Jesus,
He lives though once He died. ✍

II Samuel 23:13

ALL FAILED BUT CHRIST

I followed a religious crowd one day as they made
their way to a hill.
Soldiers seemed to protect them as they did to a
Man as they will.
I drew very close though the scene seemed so gross
I wanted to get a good view.
The Man had to be bad, I saw no one look sad as they gave
what they thought was His due.

He gave no defense and their wrath was immense.
I soon joined in with the crowd.
I looked at His chin where His beard had once been,
I too spit and did more than allowed.
The crowd must be right for the priests led the fight,
while the soldiers show valor and might.
When we reached that old hill I felt a cold chill as they
pierced His left hand, then His right.

We sat down and we looked. All His friends they forsook
the One who their hearts sought to win.
Then from that Man torn and bleeding came words far
exceeding our hatred and anger and sin.
"Father forgive" I heard very clear and once more I drew
near, for I now knew this was God's only Son
I fell to the ground. A new love I had found.
His mercy this hard heart had won.

I got up on my feet and began to repeat the
story of God's gracious Son.
Said good-bye to the crowd before Jesus I bowed my
body and mind He'd now won. ✎

8/28/04

3

AT LAST

At last I'm where I've longed to be.
I'm here on God's authority.
I see the face of Jesus now.
A multitude before Him bow.

The one who said, "I am the Vine."
With joyful sound says, "Thou art Mine."
His precious blood has set me free.
I'm His throughout eternity.

Reunion thrills my soul today.
I'm with my friends who'd warn and pray.
Pain, death and tears are unknown here.
Absent too are foes and fear.

I'm gathered with my people, like those in days of old.
We're walking on a street that's made of purest, purest gold.
But the main attraction up above,
Is the man who won us by His love.

My voice is silent down on earth.
"Jesus is worthy" - search out His worth.
Trust Him in your heart right now.
Join us in singing, to Him all bow.

Don't make me look for you in vain.
In Him you've everything to gain.
Confess your sin, and guilt and shame.
Eternal joy or endless pain. ❧

I Love You   R.S.V.P.

BETRAYED

Tree: I Peter 2:24   It is finished: John 19:30

Betrayed and forsaken He hung on that tree,
Not for sins of His own, He bled there for me.
Prophecy told us the story, the way He must die.
"Father forgive," was His very first cry.

Tomb: Luke 23:53   He is risen: Luke 24: 6

He was laid in a new tomb, guarded and sealed.
The great stone was rolled back but no body revealed.
"He is not here but is risen," the Word clearly said.

Table: I Cor. 11:23   Til He come: I Cor. 11:26

I sit at His table, gazing back to the tree,
Precious blood there was shed to save sinful me.
Tears of sorrow and joy fall fast to the ground.
I love you Lord Jesus. You sought me til found.

Throne: Rev. 5:13   Thou art worthy: Rev. 5:9

Look now to the throne, see a crown with no thorns,
King of Kings, Lord of Lords, this title He now adorns.
His subjects all bow to their Savior and Lord,
No longer rejected, worshipped, adored.

The wounded One is worthy of all my praise and song.
He paid the highest price for me, to Him I now belong.
This heart now overflows with praise,
As on His blessed face I gaze.
The Christ of the Cross is alive though once dead. ✍

Hollywood, FL   8/14/04

5

BLESSED ASSURANCE

The Holiday season has rolled away fast,
Like the leaves of a tree they really don't last.
I need something steady that won't flee away.
Perhaps the Creator will help me today.

From the very beginning He was there in the Word.
I've searched many pages, believed all I've heard.
It tells of a Man that would come from above.
He'd die on a tree—indescribable love.

But how can I reach Him and know He is real?
I've read not by works nor how I may feel.
I'll turn to the Bible it's answers are true.
When earthly things fail me He comes in full view.

He must come here to earth in a miraculous way,
Be free from all sin if man's debt He's to pay.
Oft times we would find Him in prayer on His knees,
With one object before Him, His Father to please.

Man was condemned because of his sin,
But the sent One was gentle and so pure within.
Why would He choose such horrible pain?
With His Father He planned it to remove every stain.

Let's take a view from our substitute's eye.
The reason is found in His very first cry.
"Father forgive them" He made it so clear.
He bore all our sins, we now can draw near.

I love my Redeemer, not now on the tree,
But seated in glory in royal majesty.
He's coming again and I'll see His face.
My Savior, my Savior, what undeserved grace. ❧

BREAK BREAD

The Lord plainly said I'm to break bread.
"This do in Remembrance of Me."
Putting pleasures aside it's with Him I abide.
See the suffering He bore on the tree.

Plucking hairs from His face the whole human race,
Was involved in the torture He bore.
The scourge tore His back they never did slack.
They acted like they still wanted more.

As I reached for the bread a sweet voice gentley said,
"I'm taking all this just for you."
My head dropped in shame when I heard Jesus' name.
All my sins came into full view.

I then took the cup as with Him I did sup.
What a price He did pay, took my sins all away.
Only blood shed could make me clean.
With His hands stretched out wide and that spear in His side,
From Him all my blessings I glean.

They struck Him hard on His face.
They knew nothing of Grace.
The thorns let the blood gently flow.
He cried, "Father forgive," that all sinners might live.
What mercy, patience and grace He did show.

When I drink of that cup I see Christ lifted up.
All my debt He did pay. There was no other way.
God's Word said blood must be shed.
His love was so great He ignored all the hate.
He died but He rose from the dead. ✍

I Corinthians 11:23

BY FAITH

The Bible speaks of faith in God,
Which saves man from that fearful rod.
It means to trust Him every day,
To walk with Him and to obey.

Faith by itself is only dead.
James 2:17 is where it's read,
Abraham believed God's Word,
Did all the things that He had heard.

His son upon the alter lay.
No questions asked - it was God's way.
When Isaac from His heart was given.
His father's faith knew He'd be risen.

It pictures Christ who once would die.
The 3rd day He'd be raised on high.
"Jehovah Jireh" they named the place.
For there was seen God's sovereign Grace.

For Christ would die upon a tree,
Rise from the dead to set me free.
Faith in creation is a must you see.
It's believing the God of eternity.

Abel offered the best of his flock,
While Cain brought works and only mocked.
Both knew acceptance was by blood alone,
And all Cain did could not atone.

Noah followed in that Hebrews book.
He builds an ark while others look.
The promised storm came just as said.
Enter the door or you were dead.

Enoch walked with God each day.
He heard His voice - He led the way.
Like Noah he had family too.
These chose Christ, what will you do? ❧

CAIN AND ABEL

I heard about creation done by God's own voice.
And the word You spoke to Adam and Eve when
you gave to them a choice.
Obedience kept the relationship disobedience
meant separation and death.
But I'm bent on having my own way as long as I have breath.

Abel and I believed in God, I thought that might get me through.
His faith and life soon angered me, and I, my brother slew.
The law was not yet given but there is consequence for sin.
I heard the punishment spelled out, how could I pardon win?

It came down to obedience. Blood called for vengeance here.
I never bowed but took my way. The price I paid was dear.
Abel was too perfect for my lifestyle way back then,
He offered God a sacrifice – His substitute for sin.

Perhaps my works will get me through,
for I have a beautiful spread,
But even now deep down I know my works to God were dead.
Thou shalt not, takes away my rights, what I eat is my own affair.
I'll protect it though I have to fight - to challenge God was rare.

Adam's always preaching and he won't disobey.
I just do what I think is right no matter what I pay.
I work hard – produce the choicest fruit.
Abel slays lambs from the flock - this way for me won't suit.

God is unfair, He refuses what I had.
He accepted my brother and then I was really mad.
Revenge came to mind, what should I now do?
You know the story true when I in anger my own brother slew.

Moses gave the picture in the first Book he had penned.
It points to God's salvation a love that has no end.
The first lamb saved a son by dying in his place.
It told us of the Lamb of God who'd die for the human race.

Paul writes in Hebrews of the sacrifice of Cain.
Because it wasn't God's way his offering was in vain.
He tells of righteous Abel who acknowledged sin and guilt.
His righteousness was in the Lamb whose precious blood was spilt.

Jude teaches us about the way of Cain.
Woe to the bloodless sacrifice it too was given in vain.
Peter called it precious blood, set all tradition aside.
Judas termed it innocent blood yet in his sins he died.

Cain and Abel teach a lesson,
for one with Christ will dwell.
While Cain still chose his own way.
How sad, he's now in hell. ❧

CHOOSE

Didn't read the words to the music but I sure did like the beat.
My foot and head kept a bobbin, could hardly keep my seat.
Sometimes I'd make up my own words not
knowing there was a message for me.
I drowned out my thoughts with that rockin',
made me feel so important and free.

The people I'd often sit with, under pressure day after day.
They were cool and loved rhythm music
and they always had plenty to say.
What they wore hardly fit them and their hair
had the strangest design.
But we all had one thing in common we bowed
to the change of the times.

My old friend Bill who was part of the gang,
sat alone at the far end of the table.
While we bobbed up and down to that loud beat and sound,
he was readin' a book with gold label.
My eye caught the words Holy Bible as he
tearfully read quiet and slow.
He'd found a true friend in Jesus,
with my crowd he'd no longer go.

He had such a peaceful look on his face as he turned
to the crowd I was with.
He said "Men I drank of the water of life,
I'll no longer be drinkin' that fifth."
We turned off the bobbin' music
and listened as he spoke of his Lord.
I knew what he had was the real thing and
it cut in my heart like a sword.

I remembered Mother and Daddy as they
used to take me to church.
For a while I thought about Jesus,
but my music drowned out my deep search.
If I keep on bobbin' and shakin'
I'll forget all my troubles and pain.
If I listen and heed this fair message I've life everlasting to gain.

I boldly looked at my old friends and I firmly stated a fact.
"I'm leaving you boys and your music,
by God's grace I'll never be back." ❧

8-27-04

CERTAIN BUT NOT SURE

It is written in the Word and I believe the truths I've heard.
Salvation is God's gift to sinful man.
It is strictly by His grace I shall see Him face to face.
My debt was paid by Him from whom I ran.

I read those words "<u>that you may know</u>."
It gives assurance – slays every foe.
My sins were laid upon God's Lamb.
I'm certain now that this was His own plan.

His spotless life could not atone,
For all the wrong that I had done.
His blood alone could satisfy,
For me, the lost, He came to die.

He bore the cross, that rugged tree.
His words and blood bring certainty.
They pierced those hands and feet one day.
Not one complaint did Jesus say.

He hung between the earth and sky.
He made them both but had to die.
I'm certain God is satisfied,
Christ now lives there by His side.

The cross is empty at this hour.
He left the tomb by His own power.
He bears the marks of Calvary,
I'm certain they belong to me.

He said He would come back again,
But I'm not sure as to just when.
And I'm not sure if loved ones will put me in the grave,
And I'm not sure if some very dear have trusted Christ,
I shed a tear.
I'm not sure you understand that He will take me by the hand,
And lead me to that promised land.

Now I am certain and I am sure.
My sinful self He has made pure.
When millions sing His praise aloud,
My voice will praise Him with that crowd.
I am sure! ❧

I John 5:13

CALEB'S GONE HOME

There is singing up in heaven. Caleb's voice has joined in praise.
All the Christians join their voices throughout the endless days.
It's round-up time in glory and your boy has heard his name.
He left us, 'til that morning, for the cowboy's hall of fame.

I trusted you with Caleb to raise for me a while,
And I know you're gonna miss him and that old familiar smile.
You taught him from the Bible and all he learned was true.
Now I've called him on up higher and soon I'll come for you.

You'll be caught up soon together and
I know this thrills your heart.
And you'll be there in that mansion where you'll never, never part.
Please don't be angry with Me 'cause I called him home so young.
His witness time was over. Many souls for Me he won.
And he's learning now the meaning of those hymns
he loved and sung.

While you cried out in that hallway he was in My gentle arms.
Now I have him here beside Me free from pain and all that harms.
If you could see him walking on that golden street up here.
You'd sing and praise the Savior and dry that falling tear.

I know it pulls the heartstrings when you see the chair I used.
Now the voice you heard is silent and that's such heavy news.
You labored and you taught me and showed me endless love.
Not one deed on me was wasted your reward waits up above.

You taught me from the Bible that works could never save.
A substitute was needed so God's own Son He gave.
Do you remember when I trusted and said I now have peace?
It took the blood of Jesus to assure me sins release.

Mom and Dad I have one last request and I'll tell it to you straight.
My friends and family need to trust and I'll wait at heaven's gate.
Please don't let them disappoint me, tell them more of Jesus' love.
That He died that they might join me up here in heaven above. ✌

8/2/04

In Memory of
Caleb Custer Fletcher
Date of Birth
January 17, 1992
Date of Graduation
August 1, 2004

I can do all things through Christ
which strengthened me.
Philippians 4:13

I SAW YOUR TEARS

(Written for Caleb's parents, Mike and Darlene Fletcher)

I saw your tears the other night,
And for that grief you have a right.
I took your boy from pain and grief.
To him it was such sweet relief.

I chose you to remain a while,
Another month, another mile.
But every step you take down here,
Be very sure I'm always near.

You thought he lost the fight that night.
I took him where the Lamb's the Light.
The street is made of purest gold.
The love he knows will ne'er grow cold.

He sees the face of God's own Son.
It's He for all the victory won.
Prove He who saves, can comfort too,
Show joy and peace in all you do.

I gave My Word for you to read.
By this alone you will succeed.
Stand up and face each trial, each test.
Leave all with Me for I know best.

I suffered, bled alone, and died,
That I might have him by My side.
It's fullness of joy up here above.
With smile We wait to share our love. ✍

"Whosoever liveth and believeth in Me shall never die" John 11:26
11-4-04

In recent years, Ray has been closely associated with Dunklin Memorial Camp. "Dunklin: A City of Refuge" is a tribute to the camp. Ray has written several poems about the people at Dunklin. "Mickey" is about Mickey Evans, the founder of the camp. "Who is This" is about Mary Lanier and Martha, workers at the camp.

Ray and Mickey Evans.
Ray often preaches at Dunklin.

DUNKLIN: A CITY OF REFUGE

Dunklin is known for helping man.
Those who from the truth oft ran.
Hundreds are from drugs set free.
They've found true peace and liberty.

They spent years with alcohol.
It could take months for their withdrawal.
Patience is a must indeed.
It is essential to succeed.

Brother Dunklin preached the Word.
His name at camp will oft be heard.
This man who saved so many lives,
Knew all the schemes man can connive.

This is a refuge tried and sweet.
Mickey's shelter – a safe retreat.
Where men on drugs can safely flee,
And there find life eternally.

I need no bottle nor the bar.
What I've found exceeds by far.
No staggering now, I walk so straight.
Those bondage things my soul doth hate.

All glory goes to God on high.
It's Dunklin's camp brought me nigh.
The best of men are here so long.
They leave us singing joyful song.

All praise to Jesus on His throne.
We're all one body, ne'er alone.
Eyes once dimmed with wine so red,
Have heeded what the Lord has said.

When Jesus said, "Come unto Me,
My precious blood can set you free."
I admitted wrong, my burden brought,
Learned I the sinner, have been bought.

My life no longer mine to waste.
He made the change, I did but taste.
The wasted years are in the past.
The joy now mine will ever last.

The hidden life is soon confessed.
This starts a life that's truly blessed.
Harmony among the ill, the sick,
Will cause all to much closer stick.

Love is shown beyond all measure.
Christ provides from boundless treasure.
Helpless men once criticized,
From this world were ostracized,
Now praise the Lord for liberty,
No longer bound – from sin set free.

All men are sinners. All need the Lord.
The root of the problem is oft ignored.
Drinkin' and druggin' is why they seek rest,
Ask some who have been there and now are the blessed.

I've now hit rock bottom, don't care if I live.
Can anyone help me, is there hope you can give?
All I want is my freedom from that which I'm bound.
I met one of your grads, want what he has found.

Admit you cheated, you lied, and you stole.
It's really your first step if you want to be whole.
Godly men will see you through.
Just don't you quit what'er you do.

Call it camp, rehab, or retreat,
It's where old Satan learns defeat.
It's where men's lives are turned around,
New joy and peace they sought and found.

All praise to God, to Christ the Lord.
Tho faithful men can't be ignored.
It is in Christ my hope I find.
I pleased but self - I've been so blind.
No other refuge would I seek.
I've found the Lord, the Lamb, the Meek.

Praise the Lord for Dunklin place.
I found Him here, Amazing Grace.
I'll walk and talk the Christian way,
Since my full debt He came to pay.
I fled for years but now we're one.
I'm linked with God's own spotless Son.
O blessed Lord - for you I live.
This cleansed' heart to you I give.

I sinned in thought and word and deed.
Until I found You, all I need.
Please use my lips, my hands, my feet,
Until I'm Home in Your retreat.

God created for His pleasure,
To His standard man can't measure.
We chose our will above His own,
To rescue us He left His home.

God's gift is Holy, sent from above.
He brought to earth what's known as Love.
I was by nature filled with sin.
Still, knowing this, He took me in.
Since now by blood I am His child,
I love to serve - I'm reconciled.

Had I not come to Dunklin's retreat,
My life would know ought but defeat.
Though worthless, poor, I'd sunk so low,
He brought me up from shame and woe.

We stand today where swamp once reigned.
A change was made, 'twas God ordained.
Your life can be transformed this way.
Dear Lord, for this I humbly pray. ❧

10-3-04

MICKEY

Let's give him the flowers while he's here at the camp.
We Praise God our Savior for this bright and shining lamp.
With "Others" his motto he rescues the lost.
Tells them all about Jesus disregarding the cost.

God gave him a vision of the addict's great need.
Through prayer and self-giving his plan did succeed.
Some came just to be free from their drugs,
Wound up knowing Jesus, now greet all with hugs.

A girl thought her life to be useless and wrong,
Left losing sin's burden – her heart filled with song.
A man told of being put out on the street,
No one would take him but Mickey's retreat.

Put your hand now where Jesus dwells in your heart.
Let your mind go to Calvary – your Praises will start.
I've traveled much of this old world below,
Never saw love like this preacher could show.
"Has anyone told you" I've oft heard him say,
"That God and I love you? You're invited to stay."
Those big arms embraced me, that smile I could see.
We'll soon meet in heaven, precious blood set us free.

I can picture one big "Round Up" over on that heavenly shore,
A Cowboy leads the praises in its songs forevermore.
All are smilin' as they're singin' Jesus stands in full plain view.
Mickey shouts one memorable statement
"We're all here because of You."

Dunklin's crowd just can't be counted, their joy will never cease.
Precious blood has got all present, it alone gave sin's release.
There again stands Jesus' Cowboy with a glitter in his eye,
Pointing off to Christ our Savior, "It is He who brought us nigh."

❧

23

FINAL REST

I walked the green grass of the cemetery alone,
Saw the names of some friends as I passed each headstone.
Soon others will walk where I trod today.
But under the sod will be my house of clay.

Pains gone forever, and death's in the past,
I'm happy in heaven - have a joy that will last.
Once far from the Savior, separated by sin,
I opened my heart's door, Christ came right in.

I oft was rebellious, took my own way.
He patiently waited then came in to stay.
He's ever so faithful, meets every need.
I see my Lord's face now, from all sin I am freed.

I longed for forgiveness - sought after love.
I found them in Jesus who came from above.
We walked and we talked, had sweet times of communion.
Today I'm with Him. What a blessed reunion!

Did you know God and I loved you?
It's the last time I can tell.
I'm Home now with Jesus,
Where forever I'll dwell. ✍

11-14-04

ETIQUETTE

There is always a great danger,
We'll neglect a total stranger,
Talk with only those we love,
Forgetting He was sent from God above.

Were gonna meet our loved ones soon.
It may be night or could be noon.
Together we will sing all praise.
To Jesus Christ our voice will raise.

Results of all the seed we'd sown,
Will soon be seen around the throne.
The word I spoke when at that store,
Has won that soul forever more.

Desires were changed when Christ came in.
His precious blood has cleansed all sin.
I've been accepted, loved and taught,
By the Lord - by whom I'm bought.

No more drugs nor alcohol,
Since I heard the Savior's call.
The lips that used His name in vain,
Will never more cause grief nor pain.

I was stupid, dumb and blind.
All I need in Christ I find.
My worldly friends soon left me cold.
When I stood up and spoke so bold.

Jesus saved my soul from hell.
Trust Him, He does all things well.
He promised all a Home above,
If we would change, accept His love.

I surrender heart and mind.
For He is worthy – I was blind.
Now about that man that wandered in,
Tell him of Christ who saves from sin.

God led his steps right there to you.
Show love and joy in all you do.
Peace and joy he too will find.
He'll blend his voice with yours and mine. ❧

2-1-05

GOD CHOSE SUE

Sue is a missionary in Guatemala.
She has dedicated her life to care for those children with cancer,
whose parents can no longer care for them.

Guatemala has a great, great need,
And God looks for one to please take heed.
I've searched the wide world over for a worker tried and true.
I've had so many offers but they really wouldn't do.

I need a soul to give her heart who from this world has come apart.
A girl to share her love with kids – forget herself and worldly bids.
The place I send this chosen Jewel is where she'll be for me a tool.
Cancer's struck our choicest youth;
they'll be short lived and need the truth.

Their little bodies writhe with pain,
I'll send you Sue their souls to gain.
Their swollen bodies and eyes of pain will let you
know you must remain.
Your life of sacrifice and love,
will prove you're sent from God above.
This may not be the work you'd choose,
they quickly die but need Good News.

Your tears may flow oft' like a flood,
please tell them of My precious blood.
You'll hear them cry, they'll tear your heart,
but even so they soon must part.
That boy who suffered such deep pain will
sing with you of loves refrain.
That girl for whom you shed those tears will
sing with you thru endless years.

You told them how I died for each,
your faithful message hearts did reach.
You told them how I suffered too –
a victor's crown awaits you Sue.
Thanks for all the sacrifice you made,
for every deed you'll be well paid.
Listen Sue they're singing now,
before my throne all humbly bow. ❧

I love you Sue with eternal love,
Your great reward waits up above!

GIFTS

The Christmas season brings thoughts of useful gifts.
If I get what I long for this gift my spirit lifts.
But time and nature shrinks my joy for nothing really lasts.
The clothes, the toys, the games or car are gone with winter's blast.

When funds were scarce and gifts were few,
Joy filled my heart, the smallest things would do.
Mom and Dad didn't tell me but I could see they went without,
Just so their little off springs would smile and sing and shout.

The child was getting older and heartaches it's parents gave.
But love ruled over discipline, their hope began to cave.
Let's read to the rebellious a Bible verse each day.
Perhaps it will unite us, we'll do this as we pray.

It's gifts and things my child desires so let's read about God's son.
A perfect Gift sent from above so many hearts had won.
I watched one in our family embrace this treasure dear,
And sadly watched the other bring Mom and Dad a tear.

Today my children live. But we're not one in the Lord,
Soon they will have their family and feel the piercing sword.
Wouldn't it be wonderful if all would stop and think,
And take God's gifts – His Son and life,
and from His fountain drink? ❧

"The wages of sin is death but the Gift of God is eternal life
through Jesus Christ our Lord."
Romans 6:23
"But thanks be to God which giveth us the victory
through our Lord Jesus Christ."
I Corinthians 15:57

10-23-04

GOD'S TWO SONS

Lord I'm hurting bad, I feel so sad.
You came and took my son.
He needed care and it's hard to bear,
Has death a victory won?

Friend, have you so soon forgotten,
That it was My only Son I gave,
To bring us victory o'er death and hell,
And that cold and cruel grave?

My eyes oft dim as I think of him.
That smile I just can't forget.
His voice I hear, he brought such cheer.
For me the sun has set.

Things seem so dark, he left his mark,
He knew You paid his debt.
He read your Word, believed all he heard,
Such love he'd never forget.

Can remember the night he lost life's fight,
But that's from an earthly view.
You came to his side, said
"Son come abide, I've got a mansion for you."
Now he's with the Lord whom he loved and adored,
resting safe in His care,
Waiting the day, with a shout God will say,
"Come higher My glory to share." ❧

12-5-04

I SOUGHT FORGIVENESS

I sought forgiveness with all of my might.
I did everything possible to be sure I was right.
My money, my labor, my showmanship bright.
Made me certain I got it and brought pure delight.

Conviction set in and I couldn't find peace.
Forgiveness I needed which meant sin's release.
I turned to the Bible with pages so pure.
I found what I needed and now I am sure.

I acknowledged my sin though it brought shame and grief.
Jesus' blood paid my debt and I found sweet relief.
There's room for another to find rest today.
The time is so brief don't pass it away.
From the cross came "forgive them" I can hear it's sweet sound.
Hallelujah to Jesus for His Grace did abound.

Unworthy and guilty I came to my Lord,
Confessing my sin to the one I adored.
He saw the difference, gave an embrace.
The kiss of forgiveness was placed on my face.

He could have rejected my guilty plea,
But He repeatedly said, "Come unto Me."
I came to the Savior, His hand touched my head.
But for His forgiveness, I now would be dead. ❧

I LOVE MY REDEEMER

I love my Redeemer for now I am free.
He bore all that suffering for unworthy me.
In darkness surrounded His cries there abounded.
It was written He would die on a tree.

As in the garden, He there sought my pardon.
He cared not how far He must go.
His blood must be shed He would rise from the dead.
Grace, love, and mercy combined He did show.

All the pain men could impart was only the start.
For it pleased the Lord to bruise Him.
From the scourge, nails, and spear, ugly marks now appear.
He drank that cup that was full to the brim.

Only love without end could my stubborn heart bend.
His salvation had to be free.
I was bankrupt and poor with God's judgment in store.
Who could pardon a rebel like me?

His commandments condemned me,
His wrath would soon send me,
To the punishment I really had earned.
But He came down from above to show infinite love.
He waited so long as I went with the throng.
It hurt Him as His pleadings I spurned.

Now I stand 'neath that tree, see the Man who chose me.
"Thou art worthy," I loudly proclaim.
I'll walk with the risen by His blood I'm forgiven.
I bow at His feet never more to retreat.
No sweeter sound than His name.

He said "this do" with bread and cup in plan view.
We remember His body and blood.
He finished the work from the cross did not shirk,
His atonement brings tears like a flood. ❧

I'M FREE

The mercy of God tells of pity and love.
BOTH ARE DIVINE AND SENT FROM ABOVE!
Unmeasurable, abundant, so rich and so free,
Gives hope to the sinner like you and like me.

Moses, in writing, kept mercy in view.
He gave the commandments to his people, the Jew.
Without mercy they died according to law.
It meant obedience and bondage, that's all that they saw.

Job says our sins are recorded on high.
What can erase them so we may draw nigh?
Sacrifices were offered, it took away guilt.
Even in mercy a lamb's blood must be spilt.

If you're having a trial and you've come to wits end.
Just look to the Savior, He has mercy, no end.
He's Creator, Redeemer, leave all in His hand.
We'll soon sing His praise in a far better land.

While once body and mind were subject to me.
I sacrifice all and from sin I now flee,
Am amazed at God's mercy, it drew me close to the cross.
Jesus blood there was shed to remove stain and dross.

I now shine for Jesus, I'm a child of the King.
My body and mind are the offering I bring.
The mercy God showed me, others see now in me.
Good-bye sinful deeds, from you I'm now free. ❧

IS GOD'S LAMB YOUR LAMB?

At the start of the Book, we must take a look,
In search of the Lamb that was slain.
Where "lamb" was first found, God's grace did abound.
His plan now began to be plain.

Moriah was the chosen place, and Calvary was there.
Isaac here obeyed to death a love beyond compare.
The father had the knife raised - Isaac lay quiet and still.
Can such a scene as this be our heavenly Father's will?

A substitute was needed or Isaac must needs die.
A ram caught in a thicket was the answer to his cry.
The story Moses gave to man told of God's only Son.
The knife plunged deep, God's word to keep,
the offering now was done.

In Egypt every first born required a lamb you see,
As only by the blood applied could he be spared and free.
The lamb we're told was spotless no taint without, within.
It told of Christ the heavenly Lamb who came to die for sin.

Isaiah tells a story of a Lamb to slaughter led.
The Lamb walked quietly forward not one complaint was said.
With tear filled eyes I see Him nailed to that rugged tree.
The thing that really hurt me most, what He did was due to me.

Samuel tells of a suckling lamb,
What wrong could he have done?
So soon from the womb to the merciless tomb,
For mankind a victory he won.

John tells of a lamb that was worthy of song,
To whom all praise was acclaimed.
We'll join that chorus the day's just before us,
Forever we'll tell of His fame.

John had to be true to the Word that he knew,
The wrath of the Lamb must be told.
This subject oft' silent gives hope to the violent,
God's word is more certain than gold.

The Lamb in conclusion is no mere illusion,
This Lamb is a real living friend.
Trust Him as Savior, find love without measure,
We'll praise Him where life has no end!

❧

IT'S TRUE

One day the Kingly crown He'll wear.
Never more His flesh the scourge will tear.
He hangs no more upon a tree.
He sits in Royal Majesty.

I stood, I looked, I watched Him die.
He took my place, I wondered why.
He knew His blood alone could save.
He knew He'd rise up from the grave.

His Father heard the "finished' cry.
The law, the blood, did satisfy.
The Lamb was offered once for all.
He conquered death from Adam's fall.

With bowed head I fall before this King.
I saw those scars, how could I sing?
It was my sins that caused that pain.
He did it all that I might gain.

Come with me where I once stood.
We see a blood stained cross of wood.
Redemption's work has been complete.
Death, hell, the grave know now defeat.

But another event must yet take place,
So to the tomb I must now race.
If Jesus' body lies there still,
My hope is gone, try, as I will.

One look inside that dark, dark tomb,
Removes all doubt, dispels all gloom.
Only grave clothes come in view,
The resurrection news is true.

I have a Savior, I see those wounds.
He lives, from my heart bursts glorious tunes.
The one who cleansed sin from my heart,
Now peace and comfort doth impart. ✏

IT WAS GRADUAL

The gang offered me a drink one day, but I really had no thirst.
They mocked and jeered until that day I took my very first.
A pretty girl soon offered me her companionship and charm.
The gang just laughed and said,
"Move in with her, it will do to you no harm."

A crooked business deal came up and the gang got me involved.
We could make a lot of money and our worries would be solved.
I soon became quite calloused and hardly had a friend.
My parents wept and pleaded that my life of crime would end.

The time in life was clear now and I had to make a choice.
I realized I was addicted, how I longed to hear God's voice.
I wondered if the Savior would receive a wretch like me.
I repented of my sinful ways, accepted God's salvation,
amazed that it was free.

Do you want to find this peace, and God's unchanging love?
Turn now to the Man called Jesus, whom God sent from above.
"Him that cometh unto Me I will never turn away.
I shed My blood at Calvary, it's your debt I came to pay." ❧

2-11-05

IT IS FINISHED

"It is finished," came forth loudly by the Savior on the tree.
Heaven and earth rejoiced together, for this set poor sinners free.
The punishment man deserved left man in deepest debt.
By laying down His life that day the judgments all were met.

"He is risen," said the angel there by the empty tomb.
By His glorious resurrection He gave life instead of gloom.
" I am He that liveth," the Savior now may say,
He is my close companion and I walk with Him each day.

"Til I come," brings hope – I'll be with Him very soon.
It may be early morning, it could be afternoon.
Each Lord's day at His table, memory to the cross would go.
His precious blood redeemed me, He washed me white as snow.

"Thou art worthy," are the words the blessed Savior earned.
I wasted many years of life as His boundless love I spurned.
But now the cross is empty and He sits upon His throne.
Every voice is loudly singing, "Thou art worthy, Thou alone." ❧

REDEMPTION: It is finished–on the tree–new and living way

RESURRECTION: He is risen–from the tomb–Joseph's new tomb

REMEMBRANCE: 'Til I come-at His table-New Testament in His blood

REJOICING-REIGNING: Thou art worthy-on His throne-A new song

John 19:34	Blood and water
Luke 24:6	Body
I Corinthians 11:26	Body and blood
Revelation 5:9	Blood

LOVE AND HATE

I sought to measure love and hate, I had not long to ponder.
For in His Word God plainly told how far a man can wander.
In the image of God He fashioned and formed.
But before long man his Creator had scorned.

I turned in my Bible and was stunned, sore amazed,
For there on the cross love and hate caught my gaze.
Man's hate brought forth Christ's most precious blood.
I see that stream that cleansing flood.

The nails, the scourge, the spit, the spear.
Unmeasured hate there did appear.
"Away with Him, away," they cried.
Can this be so, for these He'd die???

At first I condemned that wicked crowd.
As they spit and cursed and in mockery bowed.
Then a still small voice within me said,
"You left the Savior torn and dead."

His pleadings you ignored and shunned.
The One you mocked was God's own Son.
I saw my hate, but His love far more.
O blessed Christ, it's You I love, serve and adore. ❧

8-17-04

MAN

You were born a natural man,
Blind, dead to God, your life you ran.
Godless you pursued your way.
So careless of the price you'd pay.

In the image of God you should have been.
You chose to live a life of sin.
You are condemned, so foolish too,
You won't obey though hell's in view.

You're so far off, refuse to hear,
Satan fills your heart and ear.
It's God who calls says "Turn around."
But turn you can't! You're hooked! You're bound!

Those useless lies you have believed.
You wonder if you've been deceived.
You've joined, you've worked, cleaned up in vain,
Your deeds can offer ought but pain.

You played God from earliest days.
Your immoral life no fear displays.
Your language vile, you show no shame,
You stooped so low, blasphemed God's name.

Could you love me if this were true?
Curse God in every breath you drew?
Rebellious and corrupt you are,
No hope, just darkness, away so far.

No man from earth could save from sin,
God sent His Son your soul to win.
He took your place of shame and guilt.
He knew to save, blood must be spilt.

For every word and thought and deed,
He took the stripes, I can be freed.
Once for all your debt He paid.
This is pure love your Lord displayed.

If you were God would you seek the vile?
Would you travel far to reconcile?
Would you reach in that filth and mire?
Would you, for me, endure the fire?

The sorrow sweat and thorns He took.
He sheathed the sword. Come, take a look.
Those wounds tell all the work is done.
You trust Him now, my heart He won. ❧

11-13-04

MERCY

Psalm 107:1-43, Psalm 106:1--45

All God asks for His <u>Mercy</u> and love,
Is the Praise that is due Him, now and above.
We were hungry and thirsty and sought as a prey,
He redeemed us and fed us, let's praise Him this day,

We cried to the Lord when no help could be found.
We sat in the darkness alone and weighed down.
No one would listen nor come to our aid.
It was sin and rebellion, caused all hope to fade.

On our own we just wandered, no city in view.
All the hard things that happened were really our due.
We thought at one time our doom had been sealed.
The Lord through His Word His <u>Mercy</u> revealed.

Over rough seas we sailed through the dark deep.
The good Lord watched o'er us, our souls He did keep.
We realized His <u>Mercy</u> had kept us each day.
We'll praise Him and love Him, with Him will we stay.

Abraham's famine was a very hard test.
When the trial at last ended God showed it was best.
The prodigal son tried the pleasures of sin.
He was king of the crowd 'til His money ran thin.
God sent a famine, he no longer could roam.
His father was waiting to welcome him home.

Jonah used logic, but it wasn't God's way.
God taught him a lesson what a price he did pay.
It was <u>Mercy</u> he needed and <u>Mercy</u> was sought.
He preached in obedience, much blessing was wrought.

Job was a man with both family and wealth.
God took his children and touched on his health.
That <u>Mercy</u> so needed was abundant and free,
He overcame obstacles, God heard his plea.

<u>Mercy</u> was needed as Israel failed often.
The hunger and thirst were the hard heart to soften.
They murmured they lied, showed much discontent,
But God's hand was on them as to Canaan they went.

There are lessons we learn from the failure of friend.
The <u>Mercy</u> of God proves to be without end.
If obedient we are to the truth of God's Word.
Heartaches are avoided, let Jesus be Lord. ❧

MY REDEEMER

He made the world in which we dwell.
He came to earth His love to tell.
Man, whom He made, spurned all His grace.
They plucked the hair from off His face.

The iron He placed in hill and vale.
Man formed the spike or rugged nail.
They pierced the hands that did such good,
And no one helped they only stood.

The blind man He allowed to see,
With that wicked crowd sat silently.
The leper who was doomed to die,
Cared little for the Savior's cry.

The sick whom He restored to health,
Forgot His love and sought for wealth.
The ones He raised up from the dead,
Chose not Christ but self instead.

The deaf that couldn't hear one sound,
Failed Christ to help – not to be found.
He fed the hungry needy crowd,
He saw them spit, they mocked, they bowed.

But how about the addict folks.
So filled with drugs and dirty jokes.
Does He not care for you and me?
Must I be doomed eternally?

Perhaps today you'll hear His cry.
Trust in His love before you die.
That blood was shed upon that tree.
For useless sinners just like me.

Did I forget the adulteress one?
The forbidden act, by God, has done?
My conscience told me to abstain,
And now for me eternal pain.

That cry from Calvary – from that tree,
Cleansed all my sins and set me free.
Good-bye old world from thee I'll flee,
It's now with Christ I'll ever be. ✍

MARRIAGE

Marriage by God unites two as one.
It is clearly stated by God's only son.
It starts a new life for the couple involved.
Turn to the Bible the answers are solved.

This ordinance, divinely instituted above.
Is based on real trust and intimate love.
Not to be broken til death do us part.
Make Christ your leader from the very first start.

God gave us examples and though they be few.
Keep your eyes on the Lord, not as other men do.
It means conquering the will, loving to death.
Cleave to your partner while God gives you breath.

There is a commandment to love your own wife.
If subjection she honors it will avoid strife.
The unequal yoke is forbidden you know.
The Lord must come first, His own beauty to show.

You've taken an oath before God and man too.
It will never be broken if Christ is in view.
God will be watching each day and each night.
Perfect obedience will bring pure delight. ❧

INTRODUCTION TO
MY FRIEND PETER

Peter was raised in Sunday school, and could quote many Scriptures.

Early in his life, he became an alcoholic and lived in containers, cars or wherever he could rest. Peter had a soul, so Maurdee and I searched for him and told him God and we loved him. We invited him to a church service, to which he came.

Standing by the car door, Peter wept as we faithfully warned him about putting off the matter of his salvation.

Quoting many Scriptures, and with tears running down his face, Peter quoted, "Rum, I love, and rum I crave. Rum will carry me to my grave."

We pleaded and prayed, but his last words to us were, "Rum, I love, and rum I crave."

Within one month Peter was found dead on the dock, and about two hundred feet from where he listened to the Gospel of God's love, and how the precious blood of Christ cleanseth from all sin. He was buried, "almost persuaded."

MY FRIEND PETER

My friend Peter said:

"Rum I love, rum I crave, rum will carry me to my grave.
On my tombstone it must be wrote,
Many a gallon went down my throat."

Ray Zander's reply from the Father:

I heard a loud cry as I tried to pass by,
But that Man caught my eye on the tree.
His face was so marred that I found it too hard,
Just to follow that crowd in their glee.

The sound of the nail made my color go pale,
Such agony had never been seen.
He had power to kill but it wasn't His will,
He loved those so calloused and mean.

He cried "Father forgive," come to Me and you'll live.
I stepped forward a pace from the crowd,
Lord Jesus, I come from my beer and my rum,
If only I know I'm allowed.

As I saw all His blood tears came like a flood,
I knew that His love must be real.
He broke that old chain that gave me such pain,
To Him I give all of my zeal.

Lifted up on a tree to save sinful me,
Demands heart body and soul.
I yield all to Him – He redeemed me from sin,
Without Him I would not be whole.

48

If you're not forgiven and continue your livin'
Turn your back as He tenderly calls.
You've chosen the sorrow, there is no tomorrow,
Just darkness as eternity rolls.

Since Jesus found me new friends now surround me,
My song tells of Calvary's love.
You've all things to gain He bore all the pain,
Give Him the glory and sing that old story forever above. ✍

GUILTY

How could you show such kindness,
To a soul who walks in blindness,
When the way is clear before Him all along?

Why did you pay his terrible debt,
When you know for sure his mind was set?
Knowing what was right he chose the wrong,
Since he showed that stubborn will,
Let him seek the world's false thrill.

Let him die and let him weep and let him wail.
Lord, you're so loving, full of grace.
You knew full well what he would face.
You knew the power of your precious blood could never fail.

Your Spirit brought him to wits end,
He must confess and not defend.
That stubborn soul now couldn't flee,
I now confess that fool was me.❧

03/01/05

MY CHOICE

I praise you Lord for your boundless love,
For the grace and mercy sent down from above.
I was lost and you found me far off from the fold.
The treasures you gave me were greater than gold.

I have life everlasting; I'm free from my sin.
I opened my heart's door; the Savior came in.
I have health and I've strength and a fairly sound mind,
All the good things He offered, I had to be blind.

Taken into the family, I'm never alone.
There is but one body – the Head's on the throne.
If one member suffers, all feel the pain,
If one member's honored, we all share the gain.

A place up in heaven is assured even me.
It's hard to imagine – His own face I'll see.
The print of the nails mark His hands even now.
To you blessed Savior I humbly now bow.

His Spirit was striving 'way back when in school.
My pride kept me joking; I was but a fool.
Faithful servants oft warned me, "Trust the Lord now."
But rebellion set in, "My knee I'll not bow."

The Lord knocked so often at this stony heart,
But Satan reminds me from the things I must part.
When I saw Christ the Savior with arms stretched out wide,
I made my decision – I'll stay close by His side. ❧

NO REGRETS

There are sins I've committed, buried, ignored.
Too painful to dwell on, but known to the Lord.
The Spirit convicts, brings much guilt and deep shame.
I have no excuse; I take all of the blame.

It may be as you read this, you're one I've offended.
I ask your forgiveness, our relationship mended.
I've prayed and I've wept o'er the deeds I have done.
True repentance I own and faith in God's Son.

"Father forgive" was His cry from the tree.
Jesus forgave, Won't you do this for me?
Tell me by phone or even by mail,
I'll watch and I'll listen, please, don't you fail.

We could team up together and be strong in the Lord,
We could face the fierce battle till the day of reward.
We both owe it to Jesus who paid all our debt,
If we "LOVE" friend and foe we'll have no regret. ❧

8/23/04

OBEDIENCE HAS REWARD

Abraham was willing to yield the son he loved,
Because it was an order from the God in heav'n above.
Moriah was the chosen place, the knife would do its deed.
Isaac never faltered, as his father there would lead.

Where is the Lamb for an offering?
for someone here must die.
"God will provide," his father said,
"He will not pass us by."

Turning back a substitute was seen, he died in Isaac's place.
It was a little picture of what's known as sovereign Grace.

The one who offered Isaac now for him must seek a Bride.
His servant found Rebekah as on God he there relied.
It was her will to marry Isaac as appointed by the Lord.
The Wedding Day soon followed, they each other now adored.

This story points to Jesus who died on Calvary's tree.
His Father sent the Son He loved to die for you and me.

He too will have a Bride one day.
The church, all saved by Grace.
Won't you stop and now consider?
He longs for your embrace. ❧

10-6-04

PSALM 22

God's Holiness and love shine forth in Psalm 22.
Man's hatred and depravity come forth for us to view.
They pierced His hands, they pierced His feet,
His strength dried up from judgment's heat.

He cried My God, My God when left alone.
Blood must be shed sin to atone.
The rejected Lord was here despised.
His love was real for me He died.

Picture strong bulls surrounding a Lamb.
And the roaring of lions as they seek the I Am.
The shameless dogs and the unicorn too,
Attacked the dear Savior who hung there for you.

His cries were to God not one to the crowd.
Not one complaint as in mockery they bowed.
His bones were disjointed as the cross they did raise.
Thick darkness forbade any eye there to gaze.

The closing verse says the work is all done.
Behold He who hangs there is God's only Son.
That darkness Christ bore was all in my stead.
A shadow soon follows, He rose from the dead.

This Savior was Holy, took the title A Worm.
It was more than the nails held Him hanging so firm.
It was love without measure freely given for me.
I'll praise His name forever His own face I'll soon see.

Since all sin's punishment is now past.
You can thank Him now for His love will last.
The Savior died that all might live.
To save our souls His life He'd give. ❧

"I Am the Good Shepherd, the Good Shepherd giveth
His life for the sheep." John 10:11

PSALM 23

Psalm 23 was spoken by sheep.
The Shepherd is silent as His praises they heap.
In Psalm 22 He was pierced and denied.
Forsaken-alone, to His God He cried.

"My God, my God," sounded forth from that tree.
When this Shepherd shed blood that the sheep might go free.
Sheep are known to be lost and to wander away,
With no means of protection with their life they oft pay.

Like me they were stupid, tried to make it alone.
But the Shepherd so loved that He left heaven's throne.
Before He led sheep, He too was once led,
As a Lamb to the slaughter where His life's blood was shed.

His arms were outstretched, His feet nailed secure.
Why should He die, this Shepherd so pure?
It was dark at the cross, no eye Him could see,
As God's wrath was unleashed to save sheep like me.

It's hard to believe this good Shepherd was sold,
30 pieces of silver was the price we are told.
He created the creatures that spit in His face,
Still He loved unto death the whole human race.

Spikes pierced the hands in Psalm 22.
The sheep see the wounds, they stand out in plain view.
In Psalm 23 the rod of authority is seen,
While the staff is for strength, upon it He'd lean.

The rod speaks of power brought down from above,
While the staff is the word where we learn of His love.
Fear is distrust, we must never show doubt,
Soon in His presence we'll sing and we'll shout.

He left us His word that all may believe,
This Shepherd stands waiting for you to receive.
Psalm 23 names the Blesser, then blessings so freely bestowed,
He's the Shepherd who died, bearing sin's heavy load. ❧

PLEASE LEARN

I have sinned and confess I'm wrong.
I've lost my joy- it's squelched my song.
If I could forgiveness find,
It would bring such peace and rest of mind.

I take full blame- accuse but me.
I had a choice from sin to flee.
Tho forbidden by God's Holy Word.
I denied authority and all I'd heard.
A short lived pleasure brot such shame,
And brought dishonor to His name.

Please learn a lesson from my mistake,
Before another step you take.
The ugly scars I've left behind,
Are ever present in my mind.

If we confess, forsake, it's penned,
The Holy Word we cannot bend.
We're offered pardon from our guilt,
The blood of Christ was freely spilt.

I'm determined now to turn around,
To break the chains wherewith I'm bound.
Lord Jesus take this sin scarred frame,
And bring much honor to your name. ❧

Atlanta, GA
9-04

RICHMOND

Returned to the town where I'd spent many years,
Had times of great joy and times spent in tears.
Was there to win souls for my Lord and my King,
A godly evangelist took me under his wing.

A big house, my own business, and a car brought no peace,
My deepest desire was to have sins release.
Could quote many scriptures, name verse after verse,
To a guilty lost sinner, this made me feel worse.

If money would do it, I'd give my last cent,
But the Bible spoke clearly; I first must repent.
Was ashamed of rebellion and turning my head,
When from Jesus the Savior I constantly fled.

Am amazed at His patience, His mercy and love,
When no man could save me, He came from above.
My parents were loving and gave me the best,
But "Things" failed to satisfy, I couldn't find rest.

You can't buy salvation with silver or gold,
My Sunday school teachers thought my heart to be cold.
Christ alone saves a soul by His death on the tree,
They made it so simple, "Christ died for me!"

Jim and Betty died right after the game,
State champions we were, but things weren't the same.
The ice on the road caused their quick death,
I must find the Savior while He lendeth me breath.

Conviction set in and I searched for the Lord,
To wait any longer I couldn't afford.
The Bible had answers, I wanted one now,
I'm willing to yield, to confess and to bow.

The wages of sin is what I had earned,
God's gift through His Son I repeatedly spurned.
All alone as I sat in my car late one night,
I trusted the Savior, and had pure delight.

He shed precious blood that I might go free,
God punished His Son, for you and for me.
All the treasures I'd gathered over the years,
I yielded to Him who removed all my fears.

Lord take my heart, my lips and my feet,
That story of love please let me repeat. ❧

9-25-04

S.I.T.
(Sin-Iniquity-Transgression)

I've read about **SIN**, that it's missing the mark.
Its wages is death, leaving future so dark.
God is so Holy – can't look upon sin.
Turn back to the garden where sin entered in.

Sin brought death to Adam – his nature I own.
The law says that only shed blood can atone.
There's a way to be free from my burden and guilt.
Look off to the cross where His blood has been spilt.

I was sinking so deep in that cesspool of sin.
My only salvation – let Jesus come in.
I opened the heart's door – He came right inside.
Precious blood has now cleansed me, with Him I'll abide.

INIQUITY means willfully doing that which is wrong.
It removes all your joy – in the heart there's no song.
Described as great wickedness – crooked - perverse.
It destroys friends and families, what could be worse?

It's the misuse of a right thing, as David would show.
Job spoke of it often, as he wants you to know.
A pervert deviates from his normal behavior.
Nothing will change him but Jesus the Savior.

"Blot out all mine iniquities," was David's sad cry.
For adultery and murder the law says I die.
Messiah was promised and now He has come.
His work on the cross my freedom has won.

"I love you, Lord," this Psalmist could say,
I'm destined for Glory as my debt you did pay.
Four sons had died for the deeds I had done,
But you loved me so much you gave me your Son.

Religion may ease your conscience a day,
But only the blood can wash sin away.
You may preach, you may teach, you may sing in the choir,
Turn your eyes now to Jesus – escape judgment's fire.

I've read of **TRANSGRESSION**, it's meaning is clear,
I refused God's authority – forsook friends that were dear.
Passed over God's boundaries, did my own thing,
Disobeyed in defiance, took a pleasure mad fling.

The law says, "thou shalt not," I know that quite well,
I choose not the right way, though that could mean Hell.
Ignoring the outcome of breaking God's Word,
I have no excuse for I've read and I've heard.

Lust conquers truth, for me it's a must,
My feelings I count on, it's recorded as lust.
If I have but a moment I'll get back on course,
Am aware others waited, wound up with remorse.

I know I'm to love the good Lord 'fore I die.
I'll transgress one more season, it's for pleasure I cry.
My youth has slipped by me, its pleasures and fun.
My body more feeble, from death I can't run.
Tell my family and buddies that the choice they now make,
Could prepare them for Heaven, don't make my mistake.

Religion may ease your conscience a day,
But only his blood can wash sins away.
You can preach, you can teach, even sing in the choir,
Only Jesus can lift you out of that mire. ❧

THE CHRIST

Am I the one who mocked and jeered,
With that cruel crowd who spit and cheered?
Could I be guilty of His death,
As I watched Him take that final breath?

The hand that fed and cared for me,
Did I help nail Him to that tree?
Did my voice cry "Away! Away!"
When He was sent my debt to pay?

Did I sit down and watch Him there,
When lonely, bleeding in despair?
Was this God's only Holy Son,
Who bade us come, from whom we run?

Was my spit too upon His face,
The precious Son of God, of Grace?
Did my face show that ugly frown,
When on His head we placed a crown?

Is it nothing to you, all ye that pass by,
Won't one hear my pleading cry?
We held back nothing in our hate,
While in His hand He held our fate.

I sold this Man for some small gain,
Left now for me, eternal pain.
This Man but pities, loves, forgives,
The crucified, God's Lamb now lives.
This Man was sent from heaven above,
I would be doomed but for His love. ❧

9-22-04 Richmond, VA

THE REMEMBRANCE

What was it blessed Savior made you endure such pain and grief,
For such a wicked sinner so full of doubt and unbelief?

Your body torn and bleeding, your bones disjointed too,
WE PULLED THE BEARD FROM OFF YOUR FACE,
WE PLACED THE CROWN OF THORNS ON YOU.
What patience as we smote you,
What love shown as we slew,
I see your blood flow to the ground,
You took what was our due.

I'll break the bread this morning,
Won by that rugged cross.
I'm condemned and guilty, useless,
Your blood removed my dross.

I love you with heart undivided,
You're worthy of my all.
Thank you precious Savior,
You heard my desperate call.

This service lasts for one short hour,
You, darkness bore for three.
You hung there in the boiling sun,
Three more for sinful me.

I sit in awesome wonder as I ponder on your love,
You had to be divine Lord, sent down here from above.
Each week I'll take my place around this bread and cup,
Until I see you face to face when we are lifted up. ❧

63

INTRODUCTION TO
THE POTTER AND THE CLAY

Jeremiah 18:1-6

After reading about the potter and the clay he was molding, I drove to Williamsburg, Virginia. I watched a potter as he put a lump of clay on the wheel and allowed water in to soften the vessel.

I approached the craftsman and explained the story in the Bible. I asked if he would sell me the process from the lump of raw clay to the completed candlestick, which is what he was making that day.

The hard lump of clay was set aside and a new lump put on the wheel. As water was allowed in, he pressed and formed a vessel. The next step was to put a handle on the candlestick, and scrape a design on its side and paint the flowers.

I thanked the potter, but he said, "I'm not finished yet. The vessel must go through the fire to give it strength and beauty." After some time in the kiln, the potter presented to me a much smaller, shiny and strong candlestick.

I thought of the verses...

"He must increase, I must decrease." John 3:30

"And when thou walkest through the fire, thou shalt not be burned." Isaiah 43:2

"That the trial of your faith, being much more precious than of gold that perisheth, though it be tried with fire, might be found unto praise and honour and glory at the appearing of Jesus Christ." I Peter 1:7

God's fires do not consume, but purify the Christian!

THE POTTER AND THE CLAY
Jeremiah 18:1-6

The Potter took some clay one day,
it was useless and hard and cold.
He patiently let some water in, to soften the figure He'd mold.
"It's only fit for the junk pile," I almost let it slip,
But He turned the wheel and let it be known,
that the clay was in His grip.

It was only from earth and of so little worth,
till the Potter reached forth His hand.
He took the hard clay and He molded that day,
according to His own plan.
The clay had no beauty but He felt it his duty,
to form something shiny and strong.
The water would soften, He'd press it so often,
till an object of use came along.

I looked at the clay, turned away in dismay,
it's futile to work with this mess.
But the Potter He'd grin, let the water sink in,
His hand then started to press,
It hurt me to tears, brought sorrow and fears,
as alone I was wrought in His hand.
The things that I'd tasted, He soon crushed and wasted,
it was scary just me and the Man.

I heard the crowd "awe" at what they just saw,
for that candlestick came into view.
From that useless old mess, He made me confess,
in His hand He can make all things anew.
The Potter's a friend, and His work has no end,
and He looks for that next lump of clay.
Don't fear to say "yes" tho you've been in a mess,
the good news – He turns no one away. ✍

THE SHEPHERD AND THE SHEEP

Sheep like me are of great value,
They give meat, milk and precious wool, too.
Surely no harm can befall me,
For all of the good that I do.

I had a great day doing my own thing,
I ate and I played and I ran.
Now darkness settled around me,
Fear struck and I needed a man.

That man had to be a Good Shepherd,
One that was willing to die.
Through darkness and danger He sought me,
The shepherd – He heard my faint cry.

I ate what was right there before me,
Never thinking how far I had roamed.
No thought of that good seeking Shepherd,
Nor how many mountains He'd combed.

The enemy drew closer to me,
But the grass looked ever so green.
I'll linger a little while longer,
The dangers to me were unseen.

I saw the light of the Shepherd,
Turning night into beautiful day.
But I chose to walk on in the darkness,
No heed for the price I would pay.

I heard the roar of that lion,
As he sought after his meal.
The Shepherd shed tears o'er my body,
His love He just could not conceal.

News came that another was straying,
So the Shepherd remained in the cold.
Back home a mother was praying,
That her sheep would be safe in the fold.

The Shepherd pushed on to the lost one,
Held him tight – very close to His breast.
The lost and the straying was safe now,
The Shepherd and the sheep could have rest.

Can you imagine the joy that was waiting,
When the Shepherd walked in with His friend?
He had snatched him from death's dark cold waters,
For that Shepherd there was praise without end. ❧

December 18, 2002

Above: At the close of youth meetings in North Palm Beach, the children decorated Ray's jacket with their signatures.
Below: Ray in Israel

THE MAN WHO PAID

The man who paid that awful debt,
In agony in the Garden sweat,
Great drops of blood that fell upon the ground.
He came to pay a debt I owed,
I marvel at the love He showed,
He never stopped 'til this poor sinner He had found.
He sank into the deepest mire,
Endured God's wrath, took all the fire.

Dare I continue in my sin,
When Jesus came my soul to win?
Will I be coward or be true,
To Him who bore what I was due.
God help me to obey and do His will.

If it's mercy you need you'd better take heed,
To God's calling as what You're to do.
Admit all your sin and let Jesus come in,
And bid that bad company adieu.

Repent and confess so the Savior can bless,
He'll put a new song in your heart.
Forget all the past when your life was so fast.
It's cancelled. You have a new start

If it's fellowship you're after –to prevent a great disaster,
Be certain Christ is center- not mere man.
Trust the Lord with all your heart,
It's a perfect way to start.
Put Christ ahead of place or preacher now,
For it is clearly written He alone for you was smitten,
And its recorded "Every knee to Him shall bow." ❧

INTRODUCTION TO
TREES OF THE BIBLE

The poem, "Trees" was written after realizing it was on the third day that God created the tree, and 3 days before Christ's resurrection, He hung upon a tree.

Adam, Absalom, Haman, Zacchaeus and Jesus, all had a tree connected with their history. Peter said it was on a tree that Jesus bore our sins in his own body.

I visited the giant Sequoia National Park in California, where a car could drive through one of the trees. I also visited Muir Wood National Park and stood by a tree 367 feet high.

Ray and "General Sherman"

Ray is standing inside the giant California Redwood tree. The palms of his outstretched hands appear as white spots at the base of the tree.

TREES OF THE BIBLE

The trees of the Bible are important to all.
Upon one the answer to man and the fall.
Paul called it a cross – Peter a tree.
Christ bore there the judgment for you and for me.

From the tree the Savior made,
Man found warmth and food and shade.
On the tree where Jesus died,
The debt for sin was satisfied.

Zacchaeus was small – climbed up in a tree,
His only ambition the Savior to see.
He heard Jesus call him by his very own name,
By willful obedience he was honored by fame.

Adam was wrong when he thought he could hide,
When all God wanted was for him to abide.
He became worthy of death by fruit from one tree,
In shame and dishonor it ended his spree.

An oak took the life of Absalom we read,
Neither beauty nor wealth could make him succeed.
Haman died on the gallows his own hands had made,
His sin was found out – what a price Haman paid.

Judas was sorry they caught him that day,
He returned all the silver but that couldn't pay.
Come now to the tree of which Peter would tell,
The innocent Lamb would save me from Hell.

Nailed to the cross He would shed His own blood,
While the hatred of man came forth like a flood.
The tree is now empty He sits on a throne,
I praise my Redeemer for His blood did atone. ❧

TRAVELIN' ON

We left planet earth; we're high in the sky,
The burdens and heartaches, I bade them good-bye.
God made the heavens; I've read in His word,
His creation has beauty; I believe all I've heard.

The sun gives such warmth and the moon gives us light,
He has them in orbit, displays power and might.
God had a Son, His daily delight,
He pleased His Father, did everything right.
It must have been hard to look down on that cross,
But aside from His death, His creatures were lost.

He offered Himself so I could go free,
I can't help but love Him, He died there for me.
Thick darkness covered the scene on that day,
When Jesus, my Savior my debt there did pay.

The hands that did good they nailed to a tree,
Precious blood freely flowed sinful me now goes free.
With scarred hands He bids you, come to Him now.
Why wait any longer? Your knee you must bow. ❧

10-1-04
Atlanta to Denver

UNCONDITIONAL INDESCRIBABLE LOVE

It's early Sunday morning and my first thoughts are of Him,
The Lamb of God, the sacrifice, I see Him now but dim.

One look within I love Him more; the cross for me, He bore.
The cries I hear from that old tree cause me His love to explore.

He was daily a delight to His Father up above,
The only thing that brought him down was His eternal love.

The darkness pain and grief He bore, caused me a further look.
My sins, transgressions, and iniquities too, so willingly He took.

I see His visage marred beyond all human thought,
It pleased the Lord to bruise Him there,
This my salvation wrought. ❧

Sunday 4:OO A. M.
Dunklin Homecoming
11-28-04

INTRODUCTION TO
WHEN YOU'VE LEARNED
Deut. 33:27

"When You've Learned" was written after surgery from a World War II wound which was finally diagnosed and treated.

The hospital put me on Oxycodone and sent me home, but a severe reaction sent me back to the emergency room. They sent me to a Rehab facility where I pleaded for a shower, not having had one for 12 days.

I missed several meals and could get no one to assist in the care of the bag. I rang the bell, but no one came. I finally asked to be sent where I could take care of myself. I went to the Rehab in a wheel chair and came out with a cane.

Ray (pictured here on the right with Robert Moffet, US Marine Captain) served in the Navy aboard the flagship USS Fierce AM 97, a fleet minesweeper, during World War II. He was discharged after being wounded twice.

WHEN YOU'VE LEARNED

When you learned what it is to be lonely,
And the dearest seem far out of view,
It's time to look up and not inward,
For the Lord Himself cares for you.

When doctors, friends and family fail,
And Satan comes with his assail,
You're on your back you're all alone.
You cry to God to take you home.

It's dark and pain is ever nigh,
Strength disappears you wonder why.
You think of good days in the past,
And wonder why they couldn't last.

I'm away from my loved ones isolated, alone,
With pain and discomfort I let out a groan.
Then my thoughts leave this scene to one up above,
I see there my Savior and His unlimited love.

Lord, what happened to all those promises I read?
You said You'd be near me fear I'd not dread.
With sweet smile He whispered, "Son, I was there."
All I heard was your groaning, complaints and despair.

You forgot how deep you had sunk into sin,
And your debt that I paid or where I have been.
In creation I spoke and the work was all done,
But to save your lost soul I gave My Dear Son.

The thorns on His brow showed a trickle of blood,
The nails, scourge and spear let it flow like a flood.
"When I see the blood" the Lord spoke far away,
It provided salvation and will do so today.

On His face I see blood from the thorns deep within,
His beard was pulled out – spit dropped from His chin.
His back was torn up like a field that was plowed,
Flesh hung from His body 'twas more than allowed.

The cross is now empty – so is the tomb.
Millions have trusted – Yet there is room.
The savior's now living just as He said.
I am He that liveth though once I was dead. ✍

WHERE THERE IS GRACE
THERE IS GOVERNMENT

Genesis 6

Ark

Box

Noah built the ark of refuge,
Saved eight people from the deluge.
There was room for many more,
That which divided was a door.

We
must
enter

Exodus 12

Blood

Blood must be shed if man's to live.
A Lamb was needed, God would give.
The place of death was Calvary.
The condemned and guilty, now go free.

We
must
apply

Leviticus 1

Burnt
Offering

A burnt offering was for God alone.
The blood was shed, sin to atone.
The sacrifice comes from man's herd.
This law was written in God's Word.

We
must
obey

Numbers 21

Brazen
Serpent

Man had sinned and chosen his way,
For forty years he'd lie and stray.
One look at that serpent on the pole,
The sin sick sinner was made whole.

We
must
look

Deuteronomy 8

Bread

It took bread from heaven for man to live,
The only hope, if God would give.
He gave to all abundantly,
This promised bread to all was free. ✍

We must
gather
and eat

II Chronicles 7:14, Matthew 11:28-29

11-14-04

WHO IS THIS

If it's prayer you need, well just stop in.
If it's printing or sewing those clothes so thin.
With a smile she'll say, "Just bring them by,
I'm sure I can fix them, at least I'll try."

At the entrance to her house is love.
You knew she'd been sent from above.
She was never too busy to entertain,
When you sought Mary's help it was never in vain.

We oft times miss her on Sunday morn,
But she's off singin' about being born.
Increasing the voices that will praise the King,
When all of those Christians make heaven ring.

It seemed she knew my heart of clay,
When useless, hard and broke it lay.
Her words gave hope as I heard her say,
"I'm so glad He didn't throw the clay away."

She sang those words to Amazing Grace.
At first I blamed the entire lost race.
But soon her words reached deep within,
I saw He died <u>My</u> heart to win.

John wrote her name in his own book.
She spoke with God if close we look.
Sat at His feet and shed a tear.
Her heart was soft she drew so near.

With Mary's name came Martha, too.
God had a work for both to do.
United close in bonds of love,
This couple served the Lord above.

The work I do is for the Lord,
The hours I spend you can't afford.
Each task is done by Jesus' strength,
For Him I'll go the farthest length. ❧

WHY WAIT?

If I were God and sought your love,
And sent my Son from heaven above,
Then waited long for your reply,
I'd choose another, pass you by.

I know you're burdened with sin's debt.
I have good news, you need not fret.
My Son endured that cross of shame
For all your sins He took the blame.

Did you ever wait at someone's door?
Did the one you loved your knock ignore?
You tried to reach them through a friend.
They chose their way, they would not bend.

I had a plan so bright for you,
But I won't force nor make you do.
I gave you health and a sound mind.
That in life's turmoil Me you'd find.

You thought the world had more to give.
You shunned My love, sin's path you'd live.
Perhaps I'll call one from your home.
Or take your health so you can't roam.

When dying, quiet, upon your bed
The world will fail, no rest for head.
I'll still be pleading till you die,
You'll never say I passed you by.

I'm here with the wicked in torment and pain.
Can't someone help me, must I ever remain?
I knew about Jesus and how to be saved,
I lingered too long, now I lie in the grave.

One day I'll see Him, not as Savior, but Judge.
He'll tell how He loved me, that I wouldn't budge.
He pleaded so often through friends and His Word.
I rebelled and was stubborn, refused all I'd heard.

The family will stand by my graveside and weep.
The cold sod won't yield. My body will keep.
They'll dress me and paint me to make me look well.
Oh how will they bear it? I'm lost, I'm in Hell!

Richmond, VA
9-25-04

WHO'S GONNA
FILL THE RANKS?

Soon my generation shall see Him face to face.
We've sounded out the story; we've been saved by sovereign grace.
It's time to set your goals now, and I hope you'll live for Him.
You'll know you're on the right road when
the things of earth grow dim.

When Jesus died the apostle Paul gave Christ His rightful place.
When Moses died the ranks were filled when Joshua led the race.
Paul too has left this scene below and Timothy stepped up brave,
While Peter left the task to strangers scattered,
when silenced in the grave.

Moody, Sanky, and Billy Graham left their example
to a younger crew.
Now Caleb Flether's gone up Home and the
question now is WHO???

Who will seek to do God's will and not his own praise seek?
Who will find the ranks today and save the lost and weak?
Who would empty self and let the Lord live here within?
Who would be a vessel CLEAN and set apart from sin?

"Here am I, send me!" Do I hear one single cry?
God will bless and use you while others He'll pass by. ❧

08-08-04

WHERE IS HE?

Matthew 2:2 - First in N.T

WHERE IS THE LAMB?

Genesis 22:7

The search is on to find God's Son,
The highest place in heaven He won.
He died, He lives forevermore.
Come bow before Him - love - adore.

An angel said He now is risen,
It must be, for I'm forgiven.
Where is He, born King of the Jew?
Whose love embraces the Gentile, too

He who was God's great delight,
Who made the world by His own might.
They found Him in swaddling clothes,
They brought Him gold and all they chose.

He owned the mines from whence the gold came,
At first they honored His blessed name.
Where was He when I sank so deep in sin?
He came my wretched soul to win.

His mother saw Him on that tree,
It pierced her heart, brought misery.
Where is He? - The cross, blood stained,
But empty now the tomb remains.

But search in vain at cross or tomb remains
He is not here, heaven found Him room.
The Christ has risen and victory claimed
He lives to never die again.

82

He is my Lord, He lives to reign,
I yield my body and my mind.

He now wipes away all tears,
Removes all doubts, He calms our fears.
He rules and reigns from yonder throne,
Assures each child they're not alone.

He'll guide when life's road seems no end,
On this living Savior rely, depend.

The search is on to find God's Son.
The highest place in heaven He won.

He died, He lives forevermore.✍

HE TOOK MY PLACE

No bone could be found broken,
His blood must precious be,
Examined from all angles,
Before He hung upon that tree.

His creatures tried and killed Him,
He endured their hate and shame,
Though He had never sinned,
In love he took the blame.

The title "Lamb of God" was given Jesus here,
To qualify as Savior three things must first appear.
Precious blood, bones preserved, and pure without, within.
Who but the Lord Himself could salvation win?

His Father said He loved Him,
But He sent Him from His side.
He called Him His beloved Son,
He watched Him as He died.

Jesus looked up into heaven,
Crying "Father forgive," He paid our debt.
The entire book, the Bible,
Tells where justice and mercy met.

ON THE WAY TO THE CROSS

Lazarus was a hopeless case; he was first sick, then dead.
Death could have been avoided had Adam obeyed what God had said.
This story came from John 11 and tells us of God's plan,
The Savior must be lifted up to save poor helpless man.

This is the story of the cross, endured by God's own Son
Calvary the predicted place, where victory would be won.
I'm saved now by that precious blood shed on that cruel tree
Not long and I needed cleansing, if from sin I would be free.

I soon confessed and then forsook, I'm happy all the day.
But sadness quickly robbed that joy, tho' Christ my debt did pay.
Then Jesus comforted my heart, removed all doubts and fear,
When loved ones leave this scene below my Lord is always near.

If I'm to be a vessel used by God in His work below,
I must commune and walk with Him or fruitless I will go.
I found much to encourage tho' tribulation came my way,
"Be of good cheer, I've overcome," I hear my Savior say.

I read from John eleven on through seventeen,
And there are valued lessons I'm sure that I'm to glean.
I read of Christ's desire we'd all be Home with Him,
We'll see our Savior face to face, nothing can that vision dim.✍

JOHN 11: Lazarus-loved, sick, sleep, standing, serving, seated, loved
JOHN 12: Cross-corn and wheat (Lifted up)
JOHN 13: Cleansing
JOHN 14: Comfort
JOHN 15: Communion
JOHN 16: Cross bearing
JOHN 17: Coming glory

REMOVED: Transgressions, tarnish, tears
REVEALED: Testimony
REWARDED: Troubles, trials
REUNION: Triumph

3-5-05

85

THANKS FOR THE PHONE CALL

When you're feelin' kinda lonely,
And you don't know where to turn,
It's time to set your eyes above,
There's a lesson you must learn.

The hurts and trials that come your way,
Are well known up above.
God wants to prove He never fails,
Wants to shower you with love.

When burdened down and things get bad,
It's you I will recall.
It's deeds like this bring so much joy,
Prevent a nasty fall.

God can do without us.
But He wants us to trust Him more,
Until we hear that trumpet sound,
And forever love, adore.

Good to hear you and Bekah,
As you rode along today.
May God have full control of you,
In all you do and say.
It's great to see you young ones,
Serving God above.
What a debt we owe Him,
For all His wondrous love.❧

12-04-04

ALL FOR JESUS

Why the nails, the scourge, the spear?
What are those words from that hill I hear?
Why that deep hole sunk in the ground?
What crime in this man can now be found?

Sin has consequences, what did He do?
Witnesses lied, not just a few.
Like a Lamb, a Man's led to the place of a skull,
Of the hatred and violence there wasn't a lull.

Before even they nailed this subject to the tree,
The scourge and the rod caused the blood to flow free.
The governor who sentenced Him stated He's without sin,
But we know this had to be if our souls He would win.

The executioner who slew Him put an innocent to death,
Watched carefully and listened as He drew His last breath.
Why let mere man show such violence and hate?
Watch them taunt, beat and spit, they just couldn't wait.

The heart of God's creatures turned evil and vile,
Let's follow that crowd as they walk the last mile.
"I looked for some to take pity, but there was none."
No one more lonely than God's only Son.

"My God, My God" I hear from that tree,
Abandoned, forsaken by them and by me.
They've used the scourge; His back looked as though plowed,
The suffering they caused was far more than allowed.

His face, once revered, is now covered with blood and with spit.
How can it be, that before Him they sit?
Isn't there one who would comfort and come to His aid,
As upon that torn, bleeding body a cross was now laid?

In anger I watched as they mistreated God's Son,
Then my own heart condemned me, I would have been one.
The soldiers, the crowd, the religious were there,
As they mocked Christ the King,
a crown of thorns He would wear.

Three hours of suffering, mans cruelty unleashed,
Three hours of darkness before the Savior deceased.
No words could describe that suffering and pain,
Endured by the Savior our salvation to gain.

It's certain from scripture this was Jesus, God's Son.
His blood must be shed e'er our pardon was won.
These deeds at the cross were predicted before,
As lovingly there all our sins Jesus bore.✍

4-9-2005

Part 2
OUTLINES
AND
ACROSTICS

AS GOD SEES ME BEFORE SALVATION

Afar off from God. (Acts 2:39)

Born of the flesh. (John 3:6)

Condemned already. (John 3:18)

Dead in trespasses and sins. (Ephesians 2:1)

Enemies by wicked works. (Colossians 1:21)

Foolish. (Psalm 14:1, 53:1)

Guilty. (Romans 3:19, James 2:10)

Having no hope. (Ephesians 2:12)

Implacable (hard to convince). (Romans 1:31)

Justifying ourselves. (Luke 16:15)

Knowing not God. (I John 4:8)

Lost. (II Corinthians 4:3, Luke 19:10)

Miserable. (I Corinthians 15:19, Romans 3:16)

No fear of God. (Romans 3:18)

Obeying not the Gospel. (Romans 10:16)

Perishing. (John 3:16, II Peter 3:9, Acts 8:20)

Quenching the Spirit. (Genesis 6:3, I Thessalonians 5:19)

Resisting the Truth. (II Timothy 3:8, Romans 13:2)

Sinners. (Romans 3:23, I John 1:10)

Turned. (Isaiah 53:6, I Timothy 5:15)

Unthankful. (II Timothy 3:2, Romans 1:21)

Vessels of wrath. (Romans 9:22)

Wicked. (Psalm 7:11, Genesis 6:5)

X Excluded from heaven. (Revelation 22: 15, Luke 13:27)

Yielded to Satan. (Romans 6:13,19)

Zealous of evil works. (Romans 10:2, Titus 2:14)

REPENTANCE DEFINED

A change of mind-purpose

Knowledge of sin and guilt with deep sorrow

Turn from sin to God

Determination to break with sin and renounce it

Begin a new life of obedience and holiness

Hate sin, love life and light

Believe on, adhere to, and trust & rely on God and His Word

To reconsider

To think differently afterward

Take sides with God against yourself

Turn from iniquity and embrace the Gospel

Admit sin and guilt

Lord repented 11 times

Radical transformation of thought attitude, outlook and direction

Sorrow for fact and act and renunciation

Acceptance of Holy Spirit's enablement to holy living

Change of mind with regard to sin, self, and God

Not only sorry for my sin but sorry enough to quit

Not remorse

Before baptism

"For all have sinned and come short of the glory of God."
Romans 3:23

REPENT

Return to God and Responsibility

I Thessalonians 1:9 -How ye turned to God from idols to serve the living and true God; Deuteronomy 30:2 -Return unto the LORD thy God; Hosea 14:1 -Return unto the LORD thy God; 2 Chronicles 7:14 -If my people which are called by My name shall humble themselves and pray and seek My face and turn from their wicked way then will I hear from heaven and forgive their sin and heal their land; Isaiah 45:22 -Look unto Me; Luke 15:18-20 -I will arise and go to my father...he arose and went.

Evidence of Repentance

Job 42:61 -I abhor myself and repent in dust and ashes; Matthew 4:20 -They immediately left their nets and followed Jesus; Matthew 12:41 -Repented at the preaching of Jesus; Jonah 3: 10 -They turned from their evil way; Ezra 9:6 -I am ashamed and blush to lift up my face to Thee my God.

Punishment without Repentance

Luke 24:47 -No remission of sins; Ezekiel 18:32 -Death; Exodus 32:12 -Wrath of God; Luke 16:24 -I am tormented in this flame; 2 Corinthians 7:10 -No salvation but sorrow and death.

Examples of Repentance (9 times "they repented not.")

Matthew 12:41 & Luke 11:32 -They repented at the preaching of Jesus; Jeremiah 31:19 Surely after I was turned, I repented and after I was instructed, I smote upon my thigh. I was ashamed yea even confounded; Luke 15 -Prodigal son; I Thessalonians 1:9 -Ye turned to God from idols to serve the living and true God; Jonah 3:5-6,10 -They turned from their evil way.

Necessity to Repent

Luke 24:47 -For remission of sins; Acts 17:30 -Obey God's command; Isaiah 55:7 - Receive mercy; Jonah 3:9

Repel God's fierce anger; Matthew 4:19 -Have a true leader; I Thessalonians 1:9 - Renounce idolatry; Romans 2:3 -A void judgment; Revelation 2:3 -Receive reward; Acts 20:20 -Obey the gospel; Ezekiel 18:32 - Please the Lord.

Teachers of Repentance

Luke 13:3 -Except ye repent ye shall all likewise perish; Matthew 9:13 -(Jesus speaking) I am not come to call the righteous, but sinners to repentance; Isaiah 55:5-7 -The LORD; Acts 3:19 -Peter; 2 Chronicles 7:14 -Ezra; Acts 6:12 -The Apostles; Luke 24:47 -The Risen Christ; Romans 2:4 -Paul; Jonah 3:8 -Jonah; Mark 1:1 5 -John the Baptist; 2 Corinthians 7:10 -The Corinthian believers; Psalm 5 1:4 -King David.

FAITH (1)

Focus on the Object: Christ

Isaiah 45:22 "Look unto Me and be ye saved all the ends of the earth for I am God and there is none else." Genesis 19:17; Numbers 21:8-9; Luke 17:28-30; John 3:14; Acts 5:29-31; Hebrews 12:2

Accept Truth

John 14:6 "Jesus saith unto him, "I am the Way, the Truth and the Life; no man cometh unto the Father but by Me." John 1:17; 8:31-32; 11:26

Reconciliation-The Way
Emancipation-The Truth
Participation-The Life

Individually receive Christ as Savior and Lord

John 3:16 "For God so loved the world that He gave His only begotten Son that whosoever believeth in Him should not perish but have everlasting life." Isaiah 1:18; John 1:12; Romans 10:9

Triumph through the blood of Christ

I John 1:7 "The blood of Jesus Christ His Son cleanseth us from all sin." Hebrews 9:12,14,22; I Peter 1:18-19; Revelation 5:9

Hope in God alone

I Timothy 1:1 "Paul, an apostle of Jesus Christ by the commandment of God our Savior and Lord Jesus Christ which is our hope." Psalm 42:11; Ephesians 2:12-13; I Timothy 6:17; Titus 2:13; Hebrews 6:19-20; 1 Peter 1:3

FAITH (2)

Forget religion, tradition and feelings, & trust in the Word of God.

Acts 4:12 "Neither is there salvation in any other, for there is none other name under heaven given among men whereby we must be saved." John 20:31; I Peter 1:18-19; I John 5:13

Avoid the consequences of sin.

John 3:18 "He that believeth on Him is not condemned but he that believeth not, is condemned already because he hath not believed in the name of the only begotten Son of God." John 8:24; Romans 6:23

Intimate relationship with Christ.

John 14:21(b) "He that loveth Me shall be loved of My Father and I will love him and will manifest myself to him." Matthew 11:28-29; John 14:20; Hebrews 13:5; Revelation 3:20

Takes sides with God.

Luke 15:19 "Father I have sinned against heaven and in Thy sight and am no more worthy to be called Thy son." II Samuel 12:13; Psalm 51:4; Luke 23:40-43

Hold fast, continue, finish the course.

II Timothy 1:13 "Hold fast the form of words which thou hast heard of me in faith and love which is in Christ Jesus." John 8:31; Acts 20:24; I Timothy 1:19, 3:9, 4:13-16; II Timothy 3:14, 4:7

BAPTISM

Believers only. Acts 2:41, 8:12, 8:37, 10:48, 18:8, 19:5

Answer of a good conscience toward God.   I Peter 3:21

Practiced by first church. Acts 2:41

Testimony before the world.

Immersion. Acts 8:37-39

Symbol of what Christ went through in reality.

Manifestation that I have died. Galatians 2:20

CRUCIFIED

I am crucified with Christ.	Galatians 2:20
Christ was crucified for me.	I Corinthians 15:1
The flesh is crucified in me.	Galatians 5:24
The world is crucified unto me.	Galatians 6:14
I am crucified unto the world.	Galatians 6:14

AS GOD SEES ME WHEN SAVED

Accepted. (Ephesians 1:6)

Believer. (John 3:36, Acts 16:31)

Christian. (Acts 11: 26)

Disciple. (John 8:31)

Epistle. (II Corinthians 3:2-3)

Follower. (Matthew 4: 19)

Godly. (II Timothy 3: 12, II Peter 3:11)

Holy. (I Peter 1:15-16)

Investor. (Ephesians 5:16, Philippians 4:17)

Joyful. (I Thessalonians 5:16, Philippians 3:1, 4:4)

Kings. (Revelation 5: 10)

Lovers of God. (I Peter 1:8, 22)

Ministers. (II Corinthians 6:4)

New creatures. (II Corinthians 5:17, I Peter 2:2)

Overcomers. (Revelation 2:7-11; 3:5, 12 & 21)

Priests. (I Peter 2:5-9)

Quickened. (Ephesians 2:1,5)

Runners. (I Corinthians 9:24-26; II Timothy 2:5)

Saints. (I Corinthians 1:2, Ephesians 4:11-12)

Teachers. (II Timothy 2:2, Ephesians 4:11)

United. (I Corinthians 10:17, Ephesians 1:10)

Vessels unto honor. (II Timothy 2:21)

Worshiper. (John 4:23, Matthew 2:2,11)

X Examples. (I Timothy 1:16, I Thessalonians 1:7)

Yielded to God. (Romans 6:13-19)

Zealous of good works. (Titus 2:4)

Ray in Switzerland

Left: Ray in October 1985
Right: With Jim Price from St. Louis, a good friend
and fellow evangelist.

Thoughts on Immortality

by W. Douglas Zander

Christian Mission Press in Georgia published this
book of poems by Ray's brother Douglas in 1977.

Ray in
Key West

Ray
preaching in
Miami

Ray with
Mary Lanier
at Dunklin
Memorial
Camp in
Okeechobee,
Florida. (Mary
typed all of
Ray's poems)

RAY SHARING THE GOSPEL IN RUSSIA

Handing out
Illustrated
Bibles in the
TB Hospital

Giving a
New
Testament
to a Doctor
in Moscow

Leningrad, Russia Minesweep School (Ray had this duty in the US Navy)

His Mansion
A New
Hampshire
home for the
weary

Gospel
Meetings in
Danville,
Virginia

Longmont, Colorado

With Frank
Perry in
Spanish
Wells,
Bahamas
after a
hurricane.

With Robin Weatherford who works with the Haitian people in Abaco, Bahamas

Ray Z. With Edwin Meschket with whom he labored for years

With Rob Lindsted, Milk & Honey Ministries, Wichita, KS

Spanish Wells, Bahamas after a hurricane

Burning Cult and Occult Material in West Palm Beach

In Brooksville, Florida

At a memorial
for those who
died at
Columbine
High School

Part 3
NEW POEMS

A FRIEND LOVETH AT ALL TIMES

"There is A Friend That Sticketh Closer Than A Brother"
Proverbs 18:24

The gospel turned some souls from sin,
God blessed the place where I had been.
Christ was preached as the only way,
I made close friends that glorious day.

We studied hard that Bible Book,
For my good friends I'd always look.
Together we some souls brought in,
We had one aim, more friends to win.

We traveled 'cross this sin sick land,
We saw souls saved by God's own hand.
It bonded us so close in one,
We shared our love with God's own Son.

I won some friends at risk of death,
I praised my God for every breath.
The doctors loaded me with pills,
Souls still professed – my only thrills.

When trials hit hard and failure came,
My friends grew cold – not quite the same.
They failed to come – stand by my side,
In Christ alone I must confide.

But failure struck – hard to believe,
I looked for friends to help relieve.
A true friend loves one all the time,
Mine stood far off - they heard my crime.

If what we sow, we reap is true,
These righteous souls will get their due.
We read repent - I've been that road,
Confessed, forsook. He removed that load.

God help the one who's Judge and Jury,
Trust he'll avoid that hurtful fury.
How often should we all forgive?
A long as God allows to live.

A friend is one we seek when we're in debt,
Christ came to earth, our needs He met.
Someone must pay. The law demands.
He paid it all with outstretched hands.

Have you ever strayed or lost your way,
Or strictly to the path you'd stay?
His blood removed each guilt and stain,
Now true to Him I must remain.

I preach to addicts constantly,
The men need love not penalty.
"Without A Cause" my Lord forgave,
He left His home and came to save.

I'm a vessel marred – I'm only clay,
But the Potter molded day by day.
His hand oft' caused me tears and pain,
A clean, useful vessel He must gain.

My love ne'er changed for all my friends,
It will remain until life's end.
God filled the void with His own love,
Soon all those friends meet up above. ❧

A GREAT DECISION

I walked into a church one day so burdened with my sin,
A well dressed man was at the door and said, "Come right in."
I wanted to be unnoticed, so I sat back by the door,
Some of the people stared at me, hadn't seen me there before.

The choir sang several hymns I'd heard when just a child,
Memory seemed to haunt me, for since I've been defiled.
I felt so lonely and so wretched as my past came in full view,
A tear or two fell down my cheek as I sat there in that pew.

Mom and Dad were always with me,
When we went to hear God's Word.
They now were safe in heaven, I forgot the things I'd heard.
The preacher took the pulpit, I heard him say, "Let's pray."
I knew his prayer reached heaven,
For he asked God to have His way.

Turn please to John's Gospel, chapter 3 and verse 16,
He seemed to look right back at me, I felt wretched, vile and mean.
But then he told of God who gave His only spotless Son,
He told of the cross and precious blood, he there my heart had won

I rose up from the pew that day, the happiest man in town,
Couldn't wait to tell the world, I was lost but now am found.
If you would come just as you are, you'll not be turned away,
Tomorrow may be too late friend, so come to Him today. ❧

1-19-05

AM I CHRIST LIKE?

It's recorded I was righteous,
And a faithful shepherd too.
You read about my offering,
And what a spotless lamb must do.

My blood speaks oh so loudly,
Though shed long, long ago.
A few short years upon this earth,
And Home to heaven I'd go.

I was well known as a prophet,
And a keeper of my sheep.
I sought to do the will of God,
For Him my love was deep.

I suffered, bled and died alone,
And no one seemed to care.
I'm safe now in my heavenly Home,
Tell me friend will you be there?

This prophet, shepherd, offerer,
Was a picture of my Lord.
His death by one he loved so much,
Cannot go unexplored.

For Abel's blood demanded vengeance,
While Christ's blood speaks of peace.
If you expect to be forgiven,
Christ alone is sin's release.

My name is Able, I am Christ like,
And I'm wondering now 'bout you.
Do all know you're a Christian,
By what you say and do? ❧

ARE WE LIKE DAVID?

Did you ever think of David's sin,
And then look back where you had been?
His sin was published, all could see,
Would I feel shame if that were me?

He wrecked a close friend's family,
He fell in sin when warned to flee.
God soon exposed his wretched deed,
He then confessed, sought to be freed.

He paid a terrible price for sin,
God sought his heart, tried to come in.
His baby died, would he hear now?
Three more sons died before he'd bow.

God called his crime iniquity,
Perversion ruled, a one night spree.
God labeled his rebellion sin,
He missed the mark, how could he win?

Transgression too was David's charge,
Now all his wrongs grew oh so large.
It started when David despised God's law,
Was governed more by what he saw.

He broke a commandment clear and plain,
Suffered much loss and bore much pain.
This story is not mere history,
What's in your heart your God can see.

You can't conceal one single thought,
You fight against what you were taught.
When at last repentance came,
He confessed, forsook, took all the blame.

He cried for mercy, felt his guilt,
For God's forgiveness blood must be spilt.
Wash me, purge me, make me whole,
I've ruined lives, affection stole.

Oh make me clean, as clean can be,
I hurt you, Lord on my wild spree.
A clean heart is my request,
Salvation's joy for me is best.

It's a right Spirit now I seek,
Without Your love life's dark and bleak.
I read that if I would return,
My cries for help You would not spurn.

Now I come on bended knee,
And ask You Lord to hear my plea.
I then could be Your servant true,
Win other souls right back to You. ❧

2-25-05

BURDENED

When I could see no light in the darkness,
And that burden too heavy to bear.
How I longed for a friend to come help me,
And I cried out in my deepest despair.

I had a choice and I made the wrong one,
I thought of no one but me.
My friends failed with those I felt close to,
I'm hurtin' and as lonely as a man could ever be.

Hope vanished and I came to a standstill that day,
In despair I looked up to heaven and cried,
"Lord have mercy, I pray!"
With no one else to turn to I fell on my knees and I cried,
I heard a sweet voice from heaven saying,
"My son it's for you that I died!"

If you'll confess your sin, leave where you've been,
I'll take you just as you are.
With that voice of love coming down from above,
I knew that would be better by far.

Believing the Savior's message, I am a brand new man,
My burden of sin was gone now, a new life I for Him began.
I'd heard the voice of my Savior whose blood was shed for me,
I turned my life over to Jesus,
I'm in love with that Man of the tree.❧

2-16-05

COLORADO

Am back in Colorado where I've oft' times
preached God's Word.
How I long to learn of blessings from the
message they have heard.
Can see the snow capped mountains and soon
will be in white,
The elk and deer are plentiful and bugle within sight.

The big horn sheep descend from lofty mountain peak,
Cool water and the salt pond is what they really seek.
Am so glad God allowed me to have friends
here in the west,
But He who made these mountains does for man
what's always best.

We wonder why deep sorrow is oft mingled with His love,
We find such peace and comfort in the fact we'll
meet above.
The Creator is Redeemer and as Man has died to free,
The mountains hold such beauty, but it's Christ I
long to see! ✌

10-3-04

Dear Dad,

Do you remember the day you said you'd have to work real late?
You lied to mom and me, all we could do was wait.
We watched the clock, stood by the door,
then cried ourselves to sleep,
No matter what you've done, we'd welcome you,
Our love is sure and deep.

Mom struggles very hard to keep the family one,
If only you'd stop and think of all the harm you've done.
You used to take us all to church but your seat is empty now,
The preacher said God may take mom before He'd see you bow.

You're doin' the things you said were wrong,
I even thought of runnin' off, don't feel that I belong,
You're still the best Dad in all the world and I love you very much.
Please try to find a phone, Please try to keep in touch.

We can live on what you make 'cause we love you more than gold,
It doesn't matter 'bout the car and all the stuff you sold.
I miss your hugs and kisses and can't stand the way things are,
Is it true you were seen with another, drinking at some bar?

Mommy is so pretty, but that pain and grief she bears,
You could take away the burden if she knew my daddy cares.
Sometimes food's a little scarce, but we thank God for every bite,
We miss and talk of you each day and pray for you each night.

I'm gonna keep the door unlocked 'cause I know you miss us too.
If you should come while I'm asleep,
we could start a life that's new.
I talk to God about you and He always brings me cheer,
He's now my truest Friend and I find He's always near.❧
2-28-05

Dear Elaine,

From school days to the present, has been to me most sweet,
We've had both joys and sorrows unknown
where soon we'd meet.
I miss the yodelin' and Dave's singing as
we shared the word down here,
But soon we'll be together bringing comfort – endless cheer.

Thanks for all the good times in Hawaii and the States,
And even foreign countries, but a better place still waits.
We shall see the face of Jesus as promised in His Word,
And we'll blend our voice together,
tell the sweetest story ever heard.

Love, Ray
❧

10-10-04
Longmont, Colorado

DID YOU GET YOUR GIFT?

It was specifically selected,
Sent from far, so close inspected.
Some received and some rejected,
Some in anger pierced it through.
God wants an answer, what will you do?

Hundreds spit upon their Gift,
While others mocked, prepared to lift,
Their treasure on a tree,
One man sold His gift for such a measly fee.

Another at that celebration,
Made a clear wise declaration,
Lord remember me.
By His side one would deride and say come down,
The Bible even names that town.

Men little knew this Gift's true worth,
He came to earth of virgin birth.
He was forsaken, left alone,
Left what was His rightful throne.

What was done was all predicted,
Those bleeding stripes, I too inflicted.
What answer will I have that day?
I'll see God's Gift, have naught to say.

I could have trusted and received,
By Satan I have been deceived.
I knew this Gift was sent for me,
I chose a dark eternity.
I waited with that religious throng,
For me, for them no joyful song. ✍

11-10-04

FORGET NOT

The Savior died for you and me,
He took our guilt and penalty.
His suffering was beyond compare,
What would you do had you been there?

They all cried "Crucify" as though the Christ deserved to die,
These hands that break the bread today,
remember all He came to pay.
My heart is aching as I see the blessed Man of Calvary.

Taking blame for all I've done,
that Holy spotless, sinless One.
I'm here to bring to mind His death and resurrection,
while I've breath,
"I am He that liveth though once was dead,"
I am your Redeemer – the church's risen Head!❧

"Forget not all His benefits." Psalm 103:2

10-10-04
Longmont, Colorado

FORGIVEN

Forgiveness comes by God's mercy and grace,
It's a gift from the cross to the whole human race.
Received, or rejected it could mean certain doom,
It's power defeats death, hell and the tomb.

Paid for by a Man on Calvary's tree,
It means a poor sinner goes pardoned and free.
Our sins like a mountain, He knew and He saw,
His love was unmeasured to those condemned by the law.

"We'll not have this Man" was cried out by one,
How solemn he said this of God's only Son.
There's no other way to find forgiveness and rest,
There's but one way to heaven, receive and be blessed.

I learned a good lesson on how to forgive,
Confess and forsake is the right way to live.
A man stood and admitted before a large crowd,
"I need help, I've wronged others," he said, clear and loud.

One hundred men said, but one needed word,
"Forgiven" came forth, not one objection was heard.
No longer the guilty was fearful and bound,
Confessing, forsaking, true peace he'd now found.

Two more men found courage to stand and admit,
They too needed pardon, and said what was fit.
Again "Forgiven' echoed throughout the hall,
All charges were dropped – Forgiven by all.

Without shedding of blood, no forgiveness is given.
I gaze at the cross, see those nails deeply driven.
Blood flowed from His hands, His feet and His side,
For me He was offered, for me He there died.

John says, "God is faithful and just to forgive all of our sins."
But confession comes first if this pardon he wins.
David acknowledged his sin after Nathan exposed,
He pled for mercy and cleansing - true repentance he showed.

Forgiveness brings joy and your life will be new,
You'll be careful of words and the actions you do.
Forgiveness was given at a price beyond reach,
But Jesus in love came to die and to teach.

Seventy times seven is how much I'm to forgive,
"Even for Christ's sake" is the manner I'm to live.
"Your sins are forgiven you," could this be more plain?
He waits for your "Thank You,"
you have life eternal to gain.❧

8/20/04

GETHSEMANE

Gethsemane means an oil press,
The olive was crushed for its oil.
Here Judas sold Jesus for silver,
Satan's scheme our salvation to spoil.

He had just been rejected as Corner Stone,
But He came for a purpose, our sin to atone.
Soon He was betrayed and sold like a slave,
He showed love and mercy, Himself He now gave.

The tree He created on day number three,
Would soon hold the Savior, His blood would flow free.
Sin's heavy burden caused Jesus to fall,
With no eye to pity, on His Father He'd call.

<u>Relationship</u> with Father never ceased as Jesus knelt,
The contact with sin and rejection so deeply He now felt.
<u>Reasoning</u> "If it be possible" could be heard from the cold ground,
He'd drink that full cup if true peace would be found.

<u>Resignation</u> was heard as He surrendered His will,
He shed drops of blood, now on to Calvary's hill.
Jerusalem caused Him to weep and to cry,
For those who rejected He'd suffer and die.

He created the creatures that gave grief and pain,
But He'll suffer the cross their salvation to gain.
He made the ground where He fell on His face,
It was here He displayed His marvelous grace.

He who's very name is love,
Proved in the garden He was sent from God above.
Blood oozed from every pore as He fell on that cold ground,
His cry "O My Father" was a most mournful sound.

The darkness was so thick, no eye could Him behold,
The night air was so calm He was lonely and so cold.
The three friends that went with Him were soon found asleep,
For them He would still suffer, His love was very deep.

That relationship with Father was sweet and ever dear,
His Father never failed Him once, He removed all doubt and fear.
He knew that they He loved so much would nail Him to the tree,
So Gethsemane and Calvary He'd endure to set all free.

The agony in that garden proved His love without a doubt,
And though despised, rejected His blood would win that bout.
Jesus kneeled to pray, fell on the ground and then upon His face,
Lest I grow cold and forget this scene, His life I fain would trace.

Think from the stable to the garden and on to Calvary,
'Twas you He had upon His mind and even sinful me.
Men came with lanterns, torches, clubs and sword,
To take the spotless Son of God, the Man my heart adored.

Jesus addressed Judas, called him by the name of Friend,
With all the love shown by our Lord this traitor would not bend.
Remember Adam in a garden? Remember how he failed?
This second Adam though tempted and tried,
by grace He there prevailed.

Peter, James and John had failed the Lord they loved and served,
Jesus went a little farther, He'd take the punishment they deserved.
Jesus wanted His Father's will, what e'er the cost would be,
Gethsemane was but the starting point, they'd nail Him to a tree.

Look, here come the Roman soldiers,
temple guards and Judas with His crowd.
He never once tried to escape, held back His power,
their wicked deeds allowed.
Judas said "Greetings Rabbi" and betrayed Jesus with a kiss,
He threw the silver pieces down, but heaven's shore
he'll no doubt miss.

Peter showed some bravery when he cut off Malchus' ear,
But soon would act the coward and lie and hide in fear.
Jesus could have called a legion, 6000 men of Rome,
But rather chose to suffer to prepare for us a Home.

He came to do His Father's will, deny Himself, God's Word fulfill,
If God's love you now would see, look back to dark Gethsemane.
If assurance you would find,
it's Calvary's work gives peace of mind.
Does it matter to you all this pain,
in your sins will you still remain?

Blood must be shed or forgiveness none,
The accepted sacrifice was God's own Son.
He willingly gave His final breath,
Your choice today is "LIFE" or "DEATH!"

O thank you Jesus, Lord and King,
What love and peace to me, You bring.
I once was lost, corrupt and dead,
I flee the world, choose You instead.

My life was filled with sin and shame,
Gethsemane was not in vain.
I yield my mind, my heart, my soul,
I love You Lord You made me whole.

The Savior made His choice that night,
Now you decide, be sure you're right.
The Savior gave His all for you,
The question now "WHAT WILL YOU DO?"❧

3-20-05

GOD'S CHOICE

A Home is but a dwelling place,
Unless within we see a face.
What makes me long for heav'n above?
I'll see His face whose name is Love.

Once I lived a life of shame,
That's all changed, blessed be His name.
Each new day I wake with cheer,
I now rejoice for He is near.

Our need has been for a Director,
One who'd love, be our protector.
One who'd sacrifice and give,
Forget herself, for others live.

One who'd lead us to the Savior,
Teach us faith that knows no waver.
But who would tell of Calvary's tree,
That I might know He died for me?

Or of that empty, silent tomb,
Where Jesus cancelled doubt and gloom.
Or the true meaning of breaking bread,
That now He lives who once was dead.

And soon He'll sit upon His throne,
My heart o'er flows for He's my own.
God chose us one well qualified,
One who to self and pride had died.

Debbie yielded to God's will,
It all begin at Calvary's hill.
Friend, God has His eye on you,
He shed His blood with you in view.

He's knocking at your hard heart,
Receive Him now, He'll soon depart.
He offers life that has no end,
He's longing now your life to mend. ❧

11-17-04

GOD'S WORD

Lord, I don't want man's opinions; I only want your Word.
I must challenge information, can't believe all that I've heard.
All scripture is inspired by God, young Timothy was told,
Let's stand fast to what is written, be a soldier true and bold.

Moses gave the Pentateuch, the first five books he wrote,
They're full of truths 'bout Jesus, all honest scholars will take note.
"In the beginning God," is how the Bible starts,
To escape accountability, man from the truth soon parts.

I accept about creation, it's by faith I now believe,
God and man had sweet communion, 'til the devil man deceived.
The curse came in so quickly, inflicting sorrow, sweat, and sword,
But a man whose name was Jesus bore them all, His name ignored.

This book of books tells of man's fall and of his mortal sin,
Tells man can be forgiven, if he'll but let the Savior in.
The first time "Come" was in the book,
man had to enter, not just look.
Then there was the Lamb that died,
blood freely flowing from hands and side.

The serpent lifted on a pole,
proved Christ must die to make us whole,
Moriah's lamb took Isaac's place,
Egypt's lamb too death must face.

Isaiah's Lamb to slaughter led,
My Lamb lives though once was dead.
The day is coming praise the Lord,
We'll see the one who sheathed the sword.

The judgment's past and I go free,
God's Son the Lamb has died for me.

There are theories, speculations, these won't really do,
You need the bible, God's own Word, to make your life anew.
Forget about emotions for they don't stay the same,
If you find yourself in darkness, you've only self to blame.⮐

1-29-05

GREAT GUANA CAY

It's New Years day on Guana Cay,
My first thoughts are God's love for me.
He saved me, paid a terrible debt,
Aside from Him, I'd owe it yet.

At New years past, I joined the crowd,
No thought of God, we partied loud.
A drink, fine food, we had it all,
The music made me miss God's call.

Patiently, He waited long,
I kept amused with worldly song.
The midnight hour struck so fast,
The joy I had could never last.

I went to church when Sunday came,
Was so religious, bore no shame.
New Years comes but once each year,
O how I wish my thoughts were clear.

God speaks sometime in title wave,
Then all die, the faint, the brave.
God spared us from this terrible end,
On Him alone I must depend.

From my first visit to this land,
For Christ my Savior, I would stand.
God spoke through fire and drowning too,
While illness took away a few.

So many years have quickly passed,
Some lives were short, they didn't last.
The graveyard holds some friends I love,
They're safely Home now, up above.

God provided hope for all,
Some close their ear to heaven's call.
Some will sing through endless day,
Forever lost, some chose their way.

God gave His son for Guana's lost,
He came to earth, He knew the cost.
Christ must die upon a tree,
That shameful death was all for me.

I love you Lord, You I receive,
Your Word I've heard, I now believe.
My lips will speak but of Your love,
Until I see Your face above.❧

1-1-05

HE CHOSE TO DIE

The nails for His hands,
The spear for His side,
The thorns on His head,
He was friendless, He died.

His feet were nailed fast,
His dye was now cast,
Jesus must die on a tree,
While by law He should really go free.

I drew close, took a look at the Man God forsook,
Saw the place where His beard had once been,
There was blood and man's spit as they continually hit,
What hurt most was the innocent died for my sin.

His visage was marred, oh there hearts were so hard,
They forsook Him and everyone fled.
While alone on that tree His thoughts were of me,
I watched while His life's blood was shed.

"It is finished," I heard, thought it cruel and absurd,
That this Man, who was sinless should die.
There was no other way, for my sins He must pay.
Oh thank God I wasn't passed by!

I'll be with heaven's throng as they sing their glad song,
Of a love so abundant and free.
I'll join in that choir, He brought me up from the mire,
His precious blood cleansed even me.❧

1-2-05

HE STOOD

Should I forget Gethsemane,   **John 20:21**
And fail that love for me to see,
And not remember that cruel tree,
Where Jesus shed His blood for me.

Grant I might gaze where once He stood,   **John 20:11**
Mary's tears dried, she knew He could.
His disciples gathered full of fear,
He stood and brought them peace and cheer.

Absent Thomas lacked true faith,   **John**
    was full of doubts.   **20:24,28**
Jesus stood, showed fresh wounds
    from all His bouts.
"My Lord, My God," he said that day.
That precious blood washed all my sins away.

Those fishermen toiled all the night,   **John 21:3**
They caught no fish, not onc bitc.
Jesus stood and told them how,   **John 21:6**
He guided them, they'd listen now.   **John 21:11**

Jesus stood along the shore,   **John 21:4**
Those men were hungry, tired and poor.
He bade them come and sup with Him,   **John 21:12**
He met each need though faith was thin.

Fish for souls and earn your keep,   **John**
Feed My lambs and feed My sheep.   **21:15-16**
Follow Me, don't judge your brother, **John 21:19**
I'm in control, trust not another.

These men failed in all their quest,
Jesus fed them, gave them rest.　　**John 21:13**
They toiled for things they needed most,
He had fire, fish and bread; He was their host.

Had they looked to Him on yonder shore,
He would have met their need and give them more.
We work and scheme, make bad decisions,
When all we need are His provisions.⁊

3-27-05

HE WON MY HEART

How could one born in a stable,
Make me fit or make me able,
To stand before the Lord sent from above?
The answer isn't hard to find,
And it will bring you peace of mind,
Because His very name is Love.

He was God's spotless, sinless Son,
By dying He my heart has won.
He came to wash our sins away,
He had an awful debt to pay,
Why should He shed His precious blood,
Take all our judgment as a flood?

God's Holy eyes can't look on sin,
Christ came and stood where I had been.
For all my shame He took the blame,
O how I love Him, Praise His name.

O Lord, I long to see your face,
I'm saved alone, all by your grace.
I'm so unworthy yet accepted,
My heart o'er flows, no more rejected.

I come to you, O Gracious King,
My mind, my heart, my all I bring.
Instead of weeping, now I'll sing,
Join in the crowd, make heaven ring.❧

11-28-04

HEBREWS 10

In Hebrews 10, the Lord came down,
Bethlehem was the birth place town.
A body was prepared for Him,
He came to pay the price of sin.

The Father's will was in His heart,
From that bosom He must depart.
He watched those priests continually slay,
Christ soon would turn their night to day.

The law brought death, but He forgave.
It freed the man whom sin held slave.
Of sacrifice there was no end,
The law was firm, there was no bend.

All offerings for sins must cease,
Christ's blood alone could give release.
We have a new and living way,
Because our debt His blood did pay.

We gather now in His blessed name,
With boldness come, Removed our shame.
His promised coming brings great cheer,
The sweetest story one could hear.

Why would you turn back to sin,
When Christ came down your soul to win?
He bears the wounds, has paid your debt,
Accept God's love, your need's been met.

July 1 2004

*"The wages of sin is death, but the gift of God is eternal
life through Jesus Christ our Lord." Romans 6:23*

HOMESICK

My heart yearns for heaven's shore,
It's Christ alone I praise, adore.
My life has changed since He came in,
There's peace and joy, where once was sin.

Reunion waits for me up there,
No more sorrow I'm to bear.
No coffins, graves, nor death will dim,
My vision then, I'll be with Him.

Born of a virgin, free from sin,
He trod the road where I had been.
He qualified to take my place,
The penalty I by rights should face.

Payment, God won't twice demand,
He bears the wounds in side and hand.
O may I never lose my way,
Until I see Him, cloudless day.

The love on earth I used to share,
Will all be His when I am there.
My song then shall forever be,
Of God's own Lamb who died for me.

No longer fear of death's demands,
My Savior shows those pierced hands.
He bore sin's awful penalty,
He paid in full, I now go free.

If you this Man have not received,
Repent, believe, don't be deceived.
No love like His has e'er been shown,
His blood can save and that alone.

12-29-04

HOPE

If there really is a heaven, and I believe it's true,
I know my dear loved one is up yonder there with You.
Forgive me if I sorrow 'cause to me he was so dear,
I know the day is coming when you'll wipe away each tear.

I read about reunion with those who've gone before,
Each time I read 'bout You Lord, I long for heavens shore.
I'll see the pearly gate and the street of purest gold,
You died for sinful me, Lord, sweetest story ever told.

When I see Your face I'll rejoice like I never did before,
When I see those wounds in Your blessed hands,
I'll know You were the Door.
The crown we placed upon Your head,
let precious blood flow down.
Would I have joined that wicked crowd
and acted like a clown? ❧

2-15-05

HURRICANE FRANCES

The hurricane is raging and is drawing very near,
The winds are devastating – causing grief and fear.
I'll ride out the storm 'til the danger is o'er,
Simply trusting in Jesus, as I've oft done before.

The water's nearing my front door, I'm as helpless as can be,
I've been crying out for mercy- must pray and wait and see.
The sliding door is bulging and water's coming in,
The carpet's saturated, this battle we can't win.

If God's showing us a picture of His fury and His wrath,
We're foolish not to heed His call and choose the narrow path.

Winds exceeding 100, didn't come as just a puff,
They pounded us for hours, played havoc, they were rough.
One pillar at my entrance and my lattice blew away,
A solemn reminder that we've not long to stay.

The big tree outside my window lies twisted, broken, and green,
I watched its leaves first touch the ground, more fury to be seen.
I heard a strained root finally pop, I knew it was the end,
Its beauty, fruit and stature it no longer could defend.

A car parked next to my parking space, lies buried by a tree,
If she'd heeded the danger warning, her car would be damage free.
For days, no electricity, phone nor water
and the pressure took its toll,
The police added on a curfew while the storm continued to roll.

No planes were flying and the airport lost its roof,
Not one soul received an injury, God's faithful,
this was certain proof.

When God gives peanut butter three days in a row,
Don't you start complaining, but be thankful as you go.
Thousands are starving daily with nothing to ease the pain,
Jesus hungered and thirsted, as He died our souls to gain.

You calmed the sea and wind before,
Your power and might, I can't ignore.
If repentance it is you seek today,
I humbly bow, do what you say.

I kept looking for one bright glimmer
in that dark and threat'ning sky,
It would strengthen faith
and give more hope as I on Christ rely.
Those clouds I see keep swirling,
they're angry, respect no home,
When all life's storms have ended,
I'll be with Jesus and never roam.❧

As Hurricane Frances Roared…
Sept. 6, 2004

I TRIED

I tried the world for pleasure,
But it never satisfied.
I catered to the flesh a while,
It too real joy denied.

The devil offered me so much,
I fell for all his lies.
A one-way ticket down to hell,
Is all that wretch supplied.

I knew there was a better way,
But how could I be sure?
I wanted peace and joy and love,
For these things will endure.

There's only One who could save my soul,
I sought Him fervently.
I'm the happiest man in all the world,
I'm saved, He set me free.

I'm gonna preach Christ each day,
I'll tell the world He is The Way.
No need to die and not be saved,
Salvation's free, your debt He paid.

When you turn from all your sin,
And let this loving Savior in.
A brand new life you then begin,
And seek more souls to Him to win.

2-23-05

130

I'M BUT A SERVANT

A King had a gardener who sought to grow a special rose,
His life was much affected, "Thought he owned it," I suppose.
He daily walked the garden to see the
flower that brought much pride,
Never thinking he'd get a notice, "The flower you grew has died."

The gardener saw the buds burst forth
in the most beautiful velvet white,
He brought his friends from far and near to see this gorgeous sight.
It wasn't years that brought its end,
God used it saddened hearts to mend.
It was the King that saw its worth,
and plucked it from this evil earth.

One morning very early, this gardener walked the garden fair.
To his dismay and horror the white rose wasn't there.
He inquired throughout the courtyard as to where his rose could be,
He finally reached the King who said, "I took it Home with Me!"

You really were My servant to care for this My treasure,
You worked so hard and did your job,
My praise is without measure.
When I trust you with a child or flower to raise for Me on earth,
Please keep in mind I've a better place,
for I know that rare jewel's worth.

There were many ones to choose from,
but your rose caught My eye,
I've got it in My Home now where it'll never fade nor die.
Up here it's joy and singing, there's no parting, not a sigh,
Reunion makes things sweeter in this mansion in the sky.✍

1-26-05

I'M GLAD TO BE AN
AMERICAN CHRISTIAN

I'm just an American Christian, I bear scars from WWII,
My country was founded on the Bible,
as Godly men expressed their view.
They believed in prayer and salvation,
and were guided by God's Word.
They were strong in faith, and their trust was in their Lord.

We have a constitution and men gave their lives for this,
For many years God honored us and life was calm and bliss.
Ungodly men soon rose to power and changed what God provided,
Soon Bible, Prayer and Christian things stopped,
when atheists presided.

Those in high positions degraded the U.S.A.,
Not simply by the deeds they did, but what they had to say.
I'm glad to be an American Christian,
and by God's grace I'll be 'til death,
Until I'm in that better land, I'll praise my God for breath.

Persecution drove men from their home from far across the sea,
They landed on this peaceful shore where the gospel could go free.
Will I allow ungodly men to spoil our liberty,
Or do I pray and seek God's face in meek humility?

Men have a choice to stay and obey the laws of this great land,
If they don't like America, let them leave,
we're gonna live as God has planned.
I'm for the Bible and Prayer, and I'm here to salute our flag,
If anyone objects to this, go home and pack your bag.

God's love is to all mankind and none are counted out,
The Bible's true and precious and leaves us without doubt.
Our fathers fought for what we have, some gave their life you see,
Why then let these rebels steel from us what God gave us so free.

I'll always thank my God as I salute my flag in Liberty,
Red is for that precious blood, Christ shed at Calvary.
White is for the cleansing He did for you and me,
Blue is for our heavenly Home, where we're assured to be.❧

2-9-05

I'M SAVED

I'm saved! The precious blood has cleansed me.
I'm changed! The world can look and see,
The things that one time charmed me much,
I wouldn't do now, wouldn't touch.

But my old companions keep dropin' in,
I boldly told them I was free from sin.
At first it was mere toleration,
It soon led to a compromising situation.

I'm with my friends and they won't tell,
They mocked and laughed when once I fell.
Regrets won't take the scars away,
You do the deed, you'll have to pay.

You smeared the Savior's precious name,
If they are lost, now you're to blame.
You failed to let your light shine bright,
Repent, turn back, ahead is night.

I turned back to the Bible, as I needed rest,
Saw others too had fallen, the greatest and the best.
I fled to Jesus humbled, weak, and mild,
I felt His arms embrace me.
Heard "Welcome Home My child!"

1-29-05

JESUS ALONE

Tell me more about Jesus from heaven and return,
It's Him I long to know more of, for Him my heart doth yearn.
If ever love was manifest, it was by Him alone,
Who else would stoop so low and leave His rightful throne?

The price was clear, the suffering plain,
When Jesus came not to remain,
But pay my debt upon that tree.
I now proclaim, "He loved me."

His Father's bosom was His place,
Rejoicing always there in space.
His love caused Him to come to earth,
That I might have that second birth.

His Father's will flowed through His life,
Search through the Word, there was no strife.
Salvation's plan was put in place,
Christ died to save the human race.

His will was only to obey,
My will, will mark my destiny.
Tell me more of Jesus now,
I gladly yield, before Him bow.

I wondered why He stooped so low,
Or just how far His love would go.
I hide beneath that cruel cross,
Without His blood – eternal loss.

My lips weren't silent in this world,
When shameful things I oft unfurled.
My hands did deeds so evil – vile,
He loved me then and all the while.

I fled when Jesus bade me come,
He called so often, but I'd run.
One day I saw those pierced hands,
He paid in full the law's demands.

The eyes that look for pleasure's games,
Since seeing Him, faithful remains.
O tell me more of Jesus' love,
Don't cease 'til we all meet above.

I'll feed upon this living bread,
Rest on this Rock no fear, no dread.
This Shepherd feeds, protects and guides,
How foolish he who heart divides.

I want but Christ to have His way,
In all I do or think or say.
He loved me even unto death,
I'll praise Him while He lendeth breath.

And when we meet on heaven's shore,
I'll sing and praise Him more and more!~

"He loved me!"

10-25-04

JESUS LIVES

It is resurrection morning and through the darkness we now peer,
We've come to look for Jesus, praise the Lord He is not here.
The soldiers didn't steal Him, nor did He escape just on His own,
The answer is very clear my friend, He's seated on His throne.

He walked and talked in this old world His very hands had made,
The memory of His words and deeds from me shall never fade.
I'm rejoicing in His resurrection, in me the world sees His reflection.
I'm not the man I used to be the risen Christ has set me free.

Come see the cross where Jesus died, but in that place we'll not abide,
There's better news there at His grave, for He arose our souls to save.
Look back again at that blood stained tree, was ever there such agony?
But turn your eyes to His empty tomb,
praise the Lord for you, there's room!

Because Jesus died and lives again, He longs to be your closest friend.
Let's praise Him every day down here and on into the endless years.
This Man created heaven and earth, no mind can fathom His true worth,
He was poor and rejected here below,
we're rich and accepted He loved us so.

There's a wonderful and true story of the Christ the King of glory,
How He left His Home above, received but hate, though sought but love.
The scene has changed from black to light,
since Jesus won that glorious fight.
The tomb is empty, He's not dead, He lives, the church's risen Head.

Come! See an empty cross and tomb,
millions believed and yet there's room.
Will you go on your willful way, when Jesus' blood your debt did pay?
And what a price our Savior paid, now we go free no more afraid.
Christ our anchor is there above, our haven's sure all through His love.❧

3- 26-05

KEY WEST

O Key West, Key West, who's been favored by God's love?
What have you done with Jesus, who was sent from heaven above?
I sent My servants from earliest days with the gospel plain and true,
How that Christ died on that rugged tree, He took what was your due.

Some men preached under streetlights,
there were Bibles on fishing boats,
Some men preached in the open air,
while the worldlings sowed wild oats.
One man mistreated his family when under the influence of drink,
One night he came home with a Bible, they didn't know what to think.

He called the fearful ones together, said that things were different now,
He read to them some scriptures; every head in tears did bow.
He told how he'd found forgiveness and sought their forgiveness too,
Said he was saved by the blood of Jesus, his life he'd start anew.

Oft times you'd pass a house, all were singing hymns of praise,
How I sometimes wish we could return to those peaceful happy days.
Money was quite scarce back then, few could ever boast,
We now had Christ within our hearts, that's what mattered most.

There were those who lived the lustful life,
it was self they aimed to please,
Some suffered sin's sad consequence, wound up with dread disease.
One thing about this Savior, His love, it changeth not,
No matter what you've done before His blood can cleanse each spot.

He gave His Word, you can be sure, by God's grace you can endure,
Turn from your life of shame and sin, and let this living Savior in.
O Key west your reputation sank quite low,
while Godly men My love did show.
There were a few who received My Son,
the question now, will you be one?

O Key West, My love and grace you have spurned so long,
I've spared you from the fiercest storms,
still you mock in deed and song.
Many who loved and warned you, now lie silent in the grave,
This message hasn't changed at all, Christ came your soul to save.

4-1-05

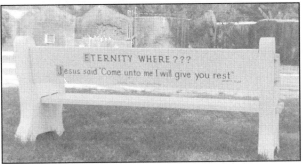

50 GOLDEN YEARS
Lawrence And Nancy

It's something to Celebrate – the 50th year,
United to one, it's time for good cheer.
It's commitment that they had in plain view,
It kept them together bonded like glue.

Can you even imagine together for 50 long years?
There's been joys, there's been sorrows coupled with tears.
It's knowing Jesus, that bonded this love,
The strength and the Grace came down from above.

If you need food or some strawberries red,
He'll toss on that hat and head for the shed.
We're so blessed by their presence, their love and their care,
We all praise the Lord for the fact they are there.

They tell of a time they knew not the Lord,
They needed forgiveness but that lion he roared.
To lose Lawrence and Nancy would ruin his game,
But they obeyed the Bible and to Jesus they came.

Him that cometh I'll not turn away,
These are the words the Savior did say.
Guilty, condemned and in need of God's rest,
They made their decision and since have been blessed.

Enter their home and they greet with a smile,
You can't help but love them when you're there for a while.
They talk of the Savior who gave sweet release,
Whose blood cleansed all sin and gave perfect peace.

If you see that old truck parked outside the door,
You know they're inside and a blessing's in store.
They are oft at the barn singing God's Praise,
To see Jesus' face they're counting the days.❧

LAWRENCE

Lawrence left us here at Dunklin for a better home above,
He obtained his heavenly passport from God's son,
His boundless love.
He trusted in the Savior who died upon that tree,
He shed His precious blood there to set all sinners free.

He didn't say good-bye to us, he only said good night,
We'll meet him soon in heaven, where the Lamb is all the light.
The street where he's now walkin' is made of purest gold,
He heard God's invitation and entered in the fold.

Lawrence served so cheerfully and faithfully here at Dunklin camp
He was a man of fervent prayer, a bright and shining lamp.
We're gonna miss his glowing smile and the things he freely gave,
He oft times spoke of Christ his Lord who came to earth to save.

I'm sure if he could speak to you at this solemn hour,
He'd tell you of the love of God, His mercy and His power.
We heard him pray so often that his family would be one,
I saw a tear roll down that cheek as he looked to God's dear Son.

Lawrence was called up from us, but the work must never cease,
O that at this hour of death, you'd trust and find relief.
It is Christ's blood alone can cleanse from every stain and sin,
Open wide your heart's door now and let the Savior in.

Now that he's in heaven he'll need that truck no more,
He's walkin' on that golden street up there on heaven's shore.
He'll be standin' there at heaven's gate to welcome Dunklin's crew
That they may join that happy choir and sing that song that's new.

I'm one of many who received from Lawrence's generous hand,
He labored hard, then gave away the fruit from God's blessed land.
He ever was so loving and thoughtful and so kind,
He entered through that pearly gate knowing REST he there would find!

1-7-05

141

LAZARUS
Sick-Sleeping-Summoned-Seated-Serving

Lazarus sat at the table,
Mary sat at His feet.
Jesus was strong and able,
Death He could conquer, defeat.

Martha went out to meet Him,
Jesus loved all three.
This family was really united,
They're one through eternity.

Lazarus lay sick and sleeping,
This sickness ended in death.
The family was grieved and broken,
But the Lord would restore to him breath.

Jesus would soon awaken,
The man who lay in the cave.
His love and His tears, His prayer and His words,
Showed He came down to save.

The purpose of this entire story,
Is to show that God's in control.
Death's in the hands of the Savior,
He gives life, defeats Satan that stole.

Mary poured out on the Savior,
The very best thing that she had.
While Judas the liar, deceiver,
Was influenced by him that was bad.

I'd love to have sat at that table,
Just to gaze on the face of my Lord.
And to be with that fortunate family,
Who entertained the One they adored.

Lazarus wound up a soul winner,
Mary learned much at His feet.
Martha served at the banquet,
Now we must this story repeat.

There's a resurrection waiting,
For all who obey that word "Come."
The precious blood shed at Calvary,
Is only accepted by some.

I'm one who now loves Jesus the Savior,
I've been bought by that man on the tree.
Why won't you too trust the Redeemer,
And from all of your sins now be free?

2:00 to 2:30 A.M.
1–10–05

The day of Lawrence Rhoden's
Graduation Celebration

LIFE

I see the clouds roll by so fast,
The leaves so green, for time will last,
Even friends with whom I dwelt,
Like winter's snow so soon will melt.

We spend our early years with care,
Soon Mom and Dad, no longer there.
The house I labored hard to get,
Has disappeared, disaster met.

The car I struggled to retain,
Soon rusted out with dirt and rain.
In the graveyard names I'd known,
I wondered when they'd read my own.

My watch and clothes and even shoes,
To someone else will be good news.
But they too soon will disappear,
Won't someone bring one word of cheer?

Is there nothing that will never die?
I've searched the world, again I'll try.
One glimpse of light I dimly see,
Life everlasting is there for me.

How may I then this life obtain,
Can I perform or pay or train?
The answer's NO, He gives life free,
His precious blood has pardoned me.

11-02-04

LUKE 23

Christ made the sun and controls its course on high,
Twelve miles per second it speeds away, one error and we'd die.
Though He controlled the universe He was led to Calvary,
The multitude accused Him and questioned violently.

They mocked Him and chastised Him, He was delivered to their will,
They derided Him, they railed on Him, He proved He loved them still.
The hands that lifted children and gave to the sick and the poor,
They now nailed to that rugged cross, His love they did ignore.

"Is it nothing to you?" Jesus cried when suffering there alone.
Five times they called Him innocent but He bled there to atone.
The day they found Him as a child they brought to Him pure gold,
But now as on the cross He hung their hearts had turned ice cold.

Away with Him, away with Him, the angry crowd did shout.
While lovingly He whispers, "Come unto me I'll never cast you out."
His Father sent Him from on high to pay the price of sin,
"Tis finished," cried God's only son, your precious soul to win.

Three languages made it very clear He was the Jew's own King,
A thief would die on either side, just one to heaven He'd bring.
They chose Barabas that sad day, they set the guilty free,
The spotless Holy Son of God was nailed upon a tree.

The awful wrath of an angry God was poured forth from above,
The darkness, pain and torment, mine, he consumed it in His love.
The centurion trusted Jesus, while Joseph His body sought,
The women prepared the spices but no need for what they brought.

The Angels gave a message that thrilled each aching one,
The Christ of God is risen, He has the victory won!❧

MERCY AND LAW

The mercy of God is oft' linked with His love,
Both are divine and are sent from above.
Immeasurable, abundant, so rich and so free,
Gives hope to the sinner, like you and like me.

God gives us commandments to show us our guilt,
No works are accepted, blood must be spilt.
We give and we labor, are baptized and attend,
Rely on God's mercy, on Him you depend.

The mercies of God are great, tender and sure,
God is the Father of all.
These mercies are said to forever endure,
Making the vilest man pure.

Some died without mercy by breaking the law,
Witnesses condemned them by what they just saw.
The law couldn't pardon, nor could it forgive,
Perfect obedience demanded if you wanted to live.

I tried my money, my friends and the Word,
The sentence was passed now, I would not be spared.
I waited, the time came, I was led to my death,
I fought and I pleaded till my very last breath.

There's a lesson to learn now, take heed while you may,
The same fate awaits you if you don't obey.
The law cannot change nor will it give in,
You sacrifice life if you're caught in your sin.❧

MY HOME

Home is where my loved ones are, and home is where I rest,
I keep in touch through God's own Word and find I'm truly blessed.
Since heaven is my final Home, I'm but a stranger here,
I have a Friend who proved His love and He is ever near.

Home is a very pleasant thought, I ponder it each day,
The fact that soon I'll see my Lord, tells me here I cannot stay.
I love the Lord with all my heart, He left His Home for me,
He came to this old sinful world to die on Calvary's tree.

Held mother in my arms the day God called her away,
Spoke her name again and again, but she heard the Lord that day.
Dad was brave as he lay dying, when leaving our weary land.
His final words "I shall know Him by the print of the nails in His hand."

Had just written to my brother when a call came he had died,
The Lord reached down and took him, safe at Home by Jesus side.
When I think of heaven I rejoice, no darkness is found there,
And pain which I've known much of, never more I'll have to bear.

Tears have often marred this face, God'll wipe them all away,
Things will be much different then, He'll turn our night to day.
I won't be mocked in my heavenly Home, no persecution there,
I'm happy now to bear His name and His rejection share.

Remove the letter "L" from world and you'll find the way to peace,
That which remains is Word and tells of sin's release.
When Jesus said, "I go to prepare a place," He spoke of Calvary,
It was there He purchased a heavenly Home for you and even me.

So Home to me means reunion and the fact I'll see His face,
The joy we'll share in that soon coming day, no man can that erase.
Have you a Home in heaven? 'Cause homes down here don't last,
Change from the world to God's own Word; God's love for you is vast.

In my early school days, we had the Bible, grace and prayer,
Ungodly men took over, they don't want these treasures there.
I used to pledge allegiance to my flag and mention God,
Foolish men fought to remove that, to let them do that, to me seems odd.

When 9-11 struck our land, we heard the call "Let's pray,"
The Tsunami took over 100,000 lives and that in one short day.
It's time we all turn back to God and on Him alone rely,
For "He that liveth and believeth in Me shall never, never die!"

2-5-05

NICK AND BRENDA

She longed for a place where that void could be filled,
I told her I found it, at the barn I've been thrilled.
These Christians show love I've never witnessed before,
They exemplify Christ who alone they adore.

I told this to Brenda she said, "I want to see,"
Quickly I offered, "Come up there with me."
We rode up together, at the barn she saw love,
Heard much about Jesus who was sent from above.

I had promised her lunch at the Indiantown Inn,
But the big church was waiting, she agreed with a grin.
The music was great and the word was sublime,
A loud voice announced, "It's love offering time."

Do I part with my dollars and lose every dime?
"Don't reach for your money," I heard a man say.
Stand up, greet a neighbor, tell 'em you love 'em,
And they are welcomed to stay.

It was now time for lunch, the dining room's full to the brim,
A young man, a youth leader, just hapt to walk in.
One seat was empty across from the blonde,
I could see very quickly, of her he was fond.

He pumped her with questions, kinda personal too,
He wasted no time her true heart to pursue.
"He's gonna phone me," she nudged me and said,
Sure enough it did happen, his mind she had read.

They prayed to the Lord to make things so clear,
There would be not a doubt, a question, a fear.
Soon Brenda asked me her wedding to share,
Devoted to Nick, his ring she would wear.

They married – are happy, Nick continues his charms,
You can tell God has blessed them by what's in their arms.
Kinsey Lyn Reynolds was God's gift to them here,
Soon brother or sister is about to appear.

We're here at this hour to devote this dear one,
To some sacred purpose for God's only son.
We pray for the day she'll trust Jesus as Lord,
Make a clear-cut commitment, make Him her adored.

Now a word for all you Mothers and each Father here today,
Be careful how you train your child, they hear each word you say.
Tell them early of salvation and the Christ of Cal-va-ry,
The Spirit will reveal the truth and through it vic-to-ry.

There are a few examples, but the best of men may fall,
Turn your eyes right now to Jesus listen to His tender call.
He'll be forever with you, so trust Him more each day,
You'll find the way to prosper is simply to obey.

God loaned you these dear little ones to raise for Him a while,
Be careful of your actions, they're gonna copy your own style.
He may let you keep 'em for one year or twenty-two,
Pray daily for His wisdom you may need more patience, too.❧

ONE WAY

Men claim to seek the Savior by their own works each new day,
They little heed the Bible, nor what the Lord may say.
There's but one way of salvation,
Still men cling to imitation.

All need a thorough cleansing by Christ's precious blood,
Only then will they find peace where joy flows like a flood.
Your giving helps the preacher get the best things here on earth,
But turn back to your Bible, these things have no eternal worth.

There is but one sure way to glory,
And it's still the same old story,
Jesus loves me this I know,
For the Bible tells me so.

Jesus said I am the Door,
But men continue to explore.
Faith alone will sure your soul,
Works will follow when you're whole.

Forget what priest or preacher said,
God's Word remains when they are dead.
Since all have sinned the Bible states,
They too must trust, he dies who waits.

You want proof your works won't do,
Turn in your Bible to Ephesians 2.
What you need is really love,
God sent Him down from heaven above.

Perhaps you yet think you can pay,
When Jesus said I Am the way.
The religious crowd is hard to reach,
They follow what the preachers teach.

Since God said you must come or die,
Open you heart's door while He's nigh.
You may say wait till tomorrow,
Waiting means eternal sorrow.

Your friends and family chose God's son,
For He alone the victory won.
Now money, works nor church won't do,
The blood of Christ was shed for you.

You may teach the Bible verse by verse,
To lose you soul what could be worse.
Your loved ones often prayed and wept,
But still God's Son you won't accept.

Some folks on emotions rest,
What sorrow when they done their best.
And hear God say you fail the test,
You won't be numbered with the blessed.

I had a place prepared for you,
You chose to sin you earned what's due.
I waited long with door wide open,
I weary grew and gave up hopin'.✎

2-15-05

REPENT

I know I broke God's holy law, my record's up on high,
But I'm hoping I can do some good – be accepted 'fore I die.
I know lots about religion, but I'm not sure which is right,
I'll start to read my Bible and work hard with all my might.

I'm reading now the Bible and it says I must repent,
Have faith in Christ the Savior and I wondered what it meant.
If I do good and change my ways will God accept me then,
Or must I humbly come to Him and on His blood depend?

I'm really sorry for my sin – it's so hard to give up,
I want the worldly pleasures – to drink from its full cup.
O how I hope that I'm all right when death does come my way,
When the judge hands down my sentence,
and I have not one word to say.

The wages of sin is stated as death,
I must turn to Jesus while he lendeth me breath.
I admit now I'm a sinner for God's word so clearly shows,
His Spirit now is striving I must repent before He goes.

I'm determined to break from my sin and my guilt,
I turn now to Jesus - for me His blood was spilt.
Or shall I wait until tomorrow and just hope that I'll be free,
His mercy is abundant now - He leaves it all to me.

Repentance will make you abhor yourself and sin,
With shame you'll bow before Him, His forgiveness you will win.
It means a leaving and a cleaving – goodbye old evil ways,
I'll cling now to my Savior – I've wasted many days.

I take sides with God – I deserve but His wrath,
I have no ground to stand on – I chose my own path.
I'll trust and rely on God's infinite love,
The transformation that's needed must come from above.

Since I had change of my heart and of mind,
His spirit now leads me – new treasure I find.
I'm not only sorry for the evil I've done,
I quit the old ways - I'm in love with God's Son.

Can you imagine the change He brought into my life,
The language – companions and lack of vain strife?
I'll rely on God's Word and I'll trust His dear Son,
My heart is now open to the work He has done.

How can I possibly continue in sin,
Since Jesus my Savior has knocked and come in?

⁊

RICK AND DORIS

Since now you chose your partner, you two shall become as one,
Be sure to start this marriage by trusting in God's Son.
Trust Him in time of plenty, for He provided all,
Trust Him in time of sorrow, He'll hear your faintest call.

It is Christ who loved you unto death, now live for Him each day,
Praise Him with your every breath, start now, please don't delay.
You have a little daughter who's watching all you do and say,
Be sure to read your Bible and live for Christ each day.

Because of Jesus' precious blood your way to heaven is free,
Thank God for His salvation, Jesus paid for all you three.
The way to live a joyful life is to be obedient to His Word,
And to put in practice all the truths that you have heard.

You are loved by all who gather, for Rick and Doris let us pray,
That God will watch and keep you in His own most loving way.
If each could make a statement and say it from the heart,
We'd thank God we are one in Christ,
from His love we shall not part.

If you ever find yourself in need, count on us to be your friend,
Jesus said that He'd be with you right to the very end.
So find your peace and love and rest in the
One who's always there,
And count on each who are here today,
their prayer and love to share.

3- 23-05

SOLDIERS OF THE CROSS

Lord I thought You to be very hard,
When You said "You sin you, you die."
But then I saw compassion,
When a friend died, I saw You cry.

It seems that every day I sin,
In word and thought and deed.
Unless You come into my life,
It's clear I never will succeed.

I watched men who once were violent,
Become "Soldiers of the Cross."
They bravely witnessed daily,
Regardless of the cost.

I wanna be like You, Lord,
And let God have my will.
And when that trumpet sounds real soon,
Lord I'm sure You'll be with me still.❧

3-6-05

THE BATTLES

YOKE   Matthew11:28,29…II Corinthians 6:14

From within and without, from below and above,
I'm fighting a battle, am returning God's love.
From within it's His <u>yoke</u> under which I now chafe,
I want my own way but I know it's not safe.

CROSS   Mark 10:21

From without it's the world, objects to me now,
I must be faithful to Christ, to Him only bow.
By His <u>cross</u> I am saved, I want all to know,
Many rebel and fierce anger they show.

THORNS   II Corinthians 14:7

From beneath, Satan hinders from the very first start,
He gives <u>thorns</u> in the flesh, hopes from Christ I will part.
Man gets puffed up and quite cold in his heart,
By God's matchless grace I'll never depart.

ROD   Proverbs 29:15…Hebrews 12:6

From above it's God's <u>rod</u> to keep my life pure,
By His precious blood I'm forever secure.
"Before God afflicted me I went astray,"
The Psalmist once penned it, it's still true today.

TRUST   Proverbs 3:5,6

Don't be discouraged, God's in control,
He can heal your weak body, He saved your poor soul.
The world, flesh, and devil will never succeed,
If you stay close to Jesus and to His word you take heed.❧

1-16-05

THE BLOOD

Acts 20 speaks of God's own blood,
The nails the scourge brought forth a flood.
It would for sin atonement give,
Blood must be shed for man to live.

In Egypt God saw blood applied,
It meant a substitute had died.
The guilty was spared well-earned death,
The spotless one took His last breath.

The river Nile to blood had turned,
Pharoah himself this plague had earned.
While plagues brought death to man and beast,
Blood of the Lamb meant life and peace,

Blood called for vengeance in the story of Cain,
Christ's blood spoke peace – He died not in vain.
Abel's lamb saved Abel the sentence of death,
He lived in obedience while God lended him breath.

When Isaac was offered there was knife, fire and wood,
Decades have passed – it's where Jesus now stood.
IIe was nailed to the cross, a spear pierced IIis side,
His blood flowed forth freely – we are now justified.

One swipe of the knife – the Lamb's blood was shed,
But Christ took the scourge while thorns pierced His head.
His life was foretold by the prophets of old,
He was even betrayed and for silver was sold.

There is no forgiveness unless blood has been shed,
You're accountable now as you've heard and you've read.
The Bible's the answer to peace and to rest,
Blood seals the transaction, praise comes from the blessed.

Peter called it precious blood, Luke gave the garden scene,
Paul said we're to remember it, John said it could redeem.
Pilate spoke of innocent blood, his wife called Jesus just,
If Jesus' face you hope to see, believing is a must.✎

THE DARKNESS

There were seven cries from Calvary,
When Jesus suffered on that tree.
In Matthew and Mark God deals with sin,
Its dark, Christ suffered deep within.

Before God tells of scourge and crown,
His fiercest wrath must first come down.
Far worse than man could ever do,
God forsook, and bruised Christ for you.

The darkness came, no eye could see,
When Jesus bore my penalty.
His love for me was so intent,
He punished Christ whom He had sent.

Forsaken means abandoned, helpless too,
Thy judgment He bore all out of view.
Predicted in Psalm twenty-two,
He took for me what was my due.

God created for His pleasure,
Suffered wrath beyond all measure.
He who's very name is Love,
Took all that wrath stored up above.

He who gave man eyes to see,
Is shut up in darkness, can it be?
The One who came to earth to save,
Dies on a cross, His life He gave.

Away, away, Him crucify,
We care not if this Man die.
Tho the one who sentenced Him to death,
Depended on Him for every breath.

Men mostly sleep when darkness come,
No rest for Christ, God's only Son.
In that dread hour my sins He bore,
He drained God's wrath, I fear no more.

"I thirst," He cried, when sun shone through,
He gave to me a life that's new.
It was plainly told, Psalm sixty-nine,
The death He died was really mine.

"Finished," was a cheerful sound,
My chains were loosed, true peace I found.
He bowed His head, went Home, above,
Can you deny that God is Love?

12-27-04

THE RIGHT TREE

Daddy, Tell me about your tree,
The one you had when young like me.
Were there lights? Had you a star? Did people come from very far?
The tree I have won't last real long,
Was your house filled with joy and song?

Son, there's quite a difference in our tree,
I came to mine on bended knee.
Your decorations got you praise,
It's on the Man I fix my gaze. Under your tree, gifts galore,
My tree offers you so much more.

At birth they brought Christ purest gold,
At death, despised, rejected, sold.
That middle tree held a great King,
To Him but nails and scourge they bring.
Memories of your tree soon will pass, Calvary's tree will ever last.

Upon your tree you put a light,
On mine, the Lord with power and might.
Son, I'm glad you did enquire,
For in my heart I've one desire.

That because of Calvary's tree,
We both believe, find liberty.
For years I too was oh so wrong,
Now in my heart He's put a song.

So glad we're His and now can sing,
Our praise our thanks to him we bring.
Son, my tree is empty now,
Let's you and me before Him bow,
Oh praise the Lord we now are one,
Forgiveness came from God's dear Son! ✍

11-12-04

161

THE TEN COMMANDMENTS

The law was given to show our guilt,
To forgive our sin blood must be spilt.
The Ten Commandments are called the law,
In them my sin was all that I saw.

In law my sins were magnified,
I had no hope, in them I died.
My mouth was stopped for guilt was seen,
Upon its justice I dare not lean.

The Law of Moses was on stone,
My works and tears could not atone.
I stand before a righteous judge,
Tho I plead or pay this law won't budge.

I confess, my sentence I have earned,
God's love and grace I often spurned.
Thought I was young, had many years,
Heard loved one plead, saw many tears.

The pleasures of sin I enjoyed far too long,
I read of God's love, oft praised Him in song.
My heart like the law was unbendable stone,
Must I wind up in hell, tormented alone?

I read of your grace back in Noah's day,
He and family were spared, all they did was obey.
You provided a door through which they were saved,
Can I flee to you now, can my sentence be waived?

You stated that blood could atone for my sin,
I repent of the past, O God let me in.
I've wasted good years, have nothing to bring,
I know for a fact I'll weep or I'll sing.

Eternity's long and you know my heart well,
If pardon you won't, I'll be cast into hell.
O God of mercies to you I now flee,
Jesus died in my place, I now can go free?

The law is good as a pattern to live,
The world can look on for a new life You give.
This body and mind, which you have made pure,
Is yours, as you bought me, your Word makes me sure.✍

12-4-04

THEY LEFT ALL

Matthew left his tax job and followed the Lord real close,
Lazarus left the dead ones and the grave clothes that were gross.
Peter left the fishing nets and turned to serve the Lord,
Paul left his religion and fought with God's own sword.

When Jesus said, "Follow me,"
Peter and Andrew from nets did flee.
Peter made it loud and clear, "We've left all," and followed near.
A woman left her water pot,
and told the men of the Christ she'd got,
Some men left parents and their home
for love of Christ and that alone.

Levi left his job and all,
when he heard the Savior's call,
James and John left mending nets,
and followed Christ with no regrets.

Simon and Andrew left casting a net,
fishers of men is the promise they get.
If my name was written, next to be read,
what of me could truly be said.

Each of the men here mentioned
made a definite change in their way,
If you truly love the Lord Jesus
you'll live for Him more every day.
What were you saved from, when Christ died in your place?
Is your light shining brightly, or are you a disgrace?

There's a sad one now I must tell you of,
A church that brought joy has left her first love.
They went on so well and had a great start,
Their failure came due to coldness of heart.✎

2-1-05

Matthew (Levi) tax collector   Mark 2:14
Peter and Andrew   Matthew 4:18-20
Peter   Mark 10:28,29
Woman and water pot   John.4:28
Parents and home   Luke 18:29
Levi's job   Luke 5:28
James and John   Matthew 4:21,22
First Love   Revelation 2:4

TODAY

Today's an important day for me,
Must keep in mind eternity.
Life is brief at the very best,
I must find peace, I long for rest.

I tried to do things on my own before,
All seemed to fail but I tried more.
When I had cash there were friends galore,
When busted and broke, was shown the door.

My family suffered, friends grew few,
Tried religion, that won't do.
Life was so lonely, filled with shame,
What hurts me most, I'm to blame.

My family, home and car I lost,
I sat and cried, how great the cost.
Thought of the days of Sunday School,
How dense I've been, I played the fool.

Who wants a "Has Been," one who failed?
Did wicked things, got caught and jailed.
A Chaplain came to my cell one day,
I'd listen well to what he'd say.

The Chaplain opened up a book,
I sat close by and took a look.
He had the Bible, told of love,
How God sent hope from heav'n above.

My heart was touched, I let Christ in,
His precious blood has cleansed from sin.
How can I prove my faith is real?
It's not by works, nor how I feel.

I'll turn from sin and company wrong,
I'll tell the truth, I'll praise in song.
I did turn, receive God's Son,
He on that cross my victory won.

For effort I would pass the test,
But I lied and cheated like the rest.
One day it all caught up with me,
I was alone, nowhere to flee.

If we'd confess, I'd read before,
Your call for help He'd not ignore.
His name is Faithful, what a Friend,
He'll stand beside you to the end.

When we were honest and obeyed,
We heard of Christ, our debt He paid.
Our hearts o'er flow with songs of praise,
We walk with Him all of life's days.

But what I did won't save your soul,
You need forgiveness to be whole.
He'll take away your guilt and shame,
Then you too can praise His name.✍

2-23-05

TWO MEN BID

Two men bid for a soul one day,
And this is what they had to say,
Both told how much they would willingly pay.
I'll give you pleasures and money and drink,
All kinds o' drugs; it'll help you to think.

I have women lined up who'll give you a thrill,
I'll work on your feelings, I control every pill.
Don't wait 'til later, come just as you are,
I'll see you at church, then we'll meet at the bar.

Your face shows you're troubled and need a good change,
I've just what you need friend, let me arrange.
Your home life is awful and you share the blame,
A little more booze, you'll forget all that shame.

When your head feels so heavy you think she'll explode,
I'll give you more drugs to lighten your load.
Ten years from today you will lie in your grave,
You'll soon be forgotten, I've made you my slave.

I lied when I told you I'd stand by you each day,
Now your soul is in torment and I planned it that way.
Your cheated, you lied, caused your family to weep,
They prayed and they pleaded but in sin you sunk deep.

I'm happy that Heaven you'll never behold,
You served Satan well; for him you were bold.
Your mother and dad are with Jesus today,
There'll be no reunion, sins wages you'll pay.

You heard the sweet story of Jesus – His love,
How all men had sinned and how He was sent from above.
I saw you were troubled, so I told you to wait,
I knew that by waiting, you'd seal your own fate.

It's time now for Jesus to come forth and tell,
How He paid all your debt to save you from hell.
By His word He can change you to live for Him here,
He offers pure water in exchange for your beer.

Good-bye to old drugs and companions that lie,
I'll make life worth livin' and give a home up on high.
You must decide now which course you will run,
The liar – destroyer or God's only Son!

WHEN GOD HAS HIS WAY

When God has His own way things prosper and there's peace,
When strife and self get in the way, the blessings soon will cease.
Looking unto Jesus is the way I ought 'a go,
By this all eyes around me will be drawn by love I show.

If Jesus stood in person and watched me through this day,
Would He be pleased with actions, and all the things I'd say?
It could be others listen and on me they have their eyes,
Would I act as I do daily or put on some disguise?

He gave me power to conform to the image He desires,
Lord help me this very day to yield as time expires.
There may not be tomorrow so the time to change is now,
Since you gave your all for me Lord right now I humbly bow.

My mind is full of God's Word and I have perfect peace,
His precious blood has cleansed me and I'm free-from sin released.
We walk and talk together and His presence is so sweet,
Stop for just a moment. This friend you now must meet.

I've grieved Him and I've hurt Him, but His love will never fail,
There's not another like Him as through this old world I sail.
Soon I'll leave this house of clay as we can't stay, but just so long,
My voice will join the singing with that happy, happy throng.
He paid my debt at Calvary and that's where I belong.❧

7/26/04
Manuel, Texas

WHERE I BELONG

If there really is a heaven,
And there's no doubt in my mind,
There's love and peace and joy up there,
More than earth could ever find.

You first took my dear mother,
Up there to be with You,
Not long, my dad soon followed,
I had heartaches not a few.

Then my brother left this scene below,
And joined in heavenly song,
I'm just markin' time down here Lord,
Soon I'll be Home where I belong.

It's hard to believe that pain and tears,
Are all up there unknown.
You paid the price and now You live,
Having earned your rightful Throne.

2-16-05

JESUS LIVES - THE GARDEN TOMB

As I drew near to the Garden Tomb, a man drew near to pray,
I saw Him fall down upon His knees, lie flay upon that clay.
I heard Him cry to His Father as He submitted to His will,
Thought His eyes looked into mine; my eyes with tears did fill.

I followed slowly to the cross that lay there on the ground,
Saw His body stretched across the wood; He uttered not one sound.
Then came the noise of that hammer,
as the nails went through each hand,
Once more those gentle eyes looked right at me,
for I had joined that wicked band.

Then soldiers lifted high that old rugged tree; dropped it in a hole,
The Man's bones were now disjointed, closer to the scene I stole.
I heard Him cry to His Father to forgive
those who caused such deep pain,
I saw precious blood flow freely, my salvation, my pardon to gain.

Thick darkness finally over, loving eyes looked down on me,
I was filled with shame and sorrow, if only I could flee!
I knew it was my sins and transgressions
caused Jesus to die on that tree,
He removed all my doubts, gave assurance, He whispered,
"I did all of this just for thee."

A granite stone one foot wide was to seal the Saviour's grave,
Eight feet in diameter couldn't stop His way to save.
Egyptian kings were mummified for all mankind to see,
At Arlington hero's bodies lie who died to set us free.
Westminster Abby holds bodies of nobility of the years,
But the Garden Tomb lies empty,
which removes all doubts and fears.

6-25-05

Part 4
NEW OUTLINES AND ACROSTICS

AN ANTHEM OF JOHN
(Outline)

A **soul** that had to be saved
A **sleep** that had to be overcome
A **stone** that had to be removed
A **service** that had to be rendered
A **sacrifice** that had to be offered
A **seed** that had to die
JOHN 12

Exodus 16 **Bread** Promised -4
Provided -14
Proclaimed -15
Personally Received -17

God's **Grace**	God's **Word**	
Redeeming	Convicts	Hebrews 4:12
Abounding	Converts	Psalm 19:7
Costly	Cleanses	John 15:3
Eternal	Conforms	John 8:31-32
	Consecrates	John 17:16-20
	Comforts	Psalm 119:50
	Corrects	II Timothy 3:16-17

Genesis
Bad Company   Bad Counsel   Bad Consequences

Noah and the Ark	**Lamb**	
Sin Reigning	Genesis 22	Power
Spirit Striving	Exodus 12	Purity
Scriptural Warning	Isaiah 53	Patience
Salvation Provided	John 1:29	Purpose
Security Extended	I Peter 1:18	Price
Service Rendered	Revelation 5:9	Praise
Sweet Savor Ascended		

C-O-M-E

COME
      C- Children
      O- Older Ones
      M- Middle Aged
      E- Everyone

COME
      C- Confidently
      O- Openly
      M- Manly
      E- Early

YOU -- COME
      C- Can
      O- Ought
      M- May
      E- Expect

FAITH CHAPTER
(Outline)

II Peter 3:5 "By the Word of God the heavens were of old, and the earth standing out of the water and in the water."

Hebrews 11:6
Creation

Substitution	Abel	Blood	Forgive
Separation	Enoch	Difference-Division	Fellowship
(Exodus 8:23)			
Security	Noah		Family
Submission	Abraham		Forsaking
Strength	Sara		Fruit

Faith-Feed-Follow-Fruit

Creation – Heaven Genesis 1
John 1 (9)Spoke   (6)Word Psalm 33 Man Genesis1:27
All Things Colossians 1:16   Glory Revelation 4:11

Remember thy Creator
Abel offered many sacrifices: to God   Testimony
Enoch (Genesis 5:22) walked: with God   To Holiness
Noah come into, warned, worked: for God
Abraham obeyed, tents: in God   Assurance
Sara Strength: by God

God requires
Saints Hall of Fame
Honor Roll O.T. Saints
Walk 8 times
Test Faith in a crucible
Work Adam and Eve saw God – worshiped, talked
Witness
Noah   Wicked warned, welcomed, worshiped, wandered

GENESIS 24
(Outline)

Well	Gospel	Prayer	Loved
House	Gift	Provision	Learned
Desert	Guide	Promise	Led
Field	Glory	Presence	Looked

Rebekah
Appointed for Isaac   14-44
Athirst
Approached   Death
Adorned   Departure
Answered   Exodus
Arose   Accomplishment
Anticipated   Taking Away
At Home   Home Coming
Admired

MY SINS ARE GONE
(Outline)

I John 2:12   "I write unto you little children because your sins
                ARE <u>forgiven</u> you for His name's sake."
Ephesians 1:7
Colossians 1:14

I John 1:7   "The blood <u>cleanseth</u> us from all sin."
Psalm 85:2   "Thou hast <u>forgiven</u> the iniquity of thy people"
               "Thou hast <u>covered</u> all their sin. Selah."

Isaiah 40:2

Psalm 103:12 "As far as the east is from the west,
             so far hath He <u>removed</u> our transgressions from us"
             12,000 miles from the north to south poles

Hosea 13:12   "The iniquity of Ephraim is <u>bound up</u> his sin is <u>hid</u>"

Hebrews 10:17 "Their sins & iniquities will I <u>remember no more</u>."

          Forgotten, Never recall or be mindful of

Isaiah 44:22   "I have <u>blotted out</u> as a thick cloud, thy
              transgressions and as a cloud thy sin.

    Swept aside, wiped out, dissipated, vapor, vanished.

Micah 7:19   "Thou wilt cast all of their sins <u>into the depths of
              the sea</u>."
            Burying our sins sea deep.

Isaiah 38:17   "Thou hast cast all my sins <u>behind thy back</u>."
Ezekiel 33:16 "<u>None</u> of his sins which he hath committed shall be
              <u>mentioned</u> unto him."
Job 14:17   "My transgression is <u>sealed up in a bag</u>."

            Package, sack, casket